CLARKSON

CLARKSON
Look who's back

GWEN RUSSELL

JOHN BLAKE

Published by John Blake Publishing Ltd,
3 Bramber Court, 2 Bramber Road,
London W14 9PB, England

www.johnblakebooks.com

www.facebook.com/johnblakebooks 🄵
twitter.com/jblakebooks 🄴

Published in paperback as Jeremy Clarkson – The Biography in 2007 and 2010,
and as Jeremy Clarkson – The Gloves are Off in 2015
This edition published in paperback in 2017

ISBN: 978 1 78606 224 6

British Library Cataloguing–in–Publication Data:

A catalogue record for this book is available from the British Library.

Design by www.envydesign.co.uk

Printed in Great Britain by CPI Group (UK) Ltd

1 3 5 7 9 10 8 6 4 2

Papers used by John Blake Publishing are natural, recyclable products made from
wood grown in sustainable forests. The manufacturing processes conform to the
environmental regulations of the country of origin.

Every attempt has been made to contact the relevant copyright–holders, but some
were unobtainable. We would be grateful if the appropriate people could contact us.

John Blake Publishing is an imprint of Bonnier Publishing.
www.bonnierpublishing.co.uk

CONTENTS

CHAPTER 1	**A MOTORMOUTH IS BORN**	1
CHAPTER 2	**THE RISE OF A LAD**	19
CHAPTER 3	**MARRIAGE & MOTORS**	37
CHAPTER 4	**STRAIGHT TALKING**	49
CHAPTER 5	**KING OF THE ROAD**	67
CHAPTER 6	**LIFE IN THE FAST LANE**	85
CHAPTER 7	**A SUDDEN CHANGE OF GEAR**	103
CHAPTER 8	**A REGULAR GUY**	123
CHAPTER 9	**BACK TO THE FUTURE**	141
CHAPTER 10	**CLARKSON STRIDES OUT**	159
CHAPTER 11	**WHO DO YOU THINK YOU ARE?**	177

CHAPTER 12 **'AWARDS NIGHTS ARE JUST
            A LOAD OF BLONDE GIRLS WITH
            THEIR BOOB JOBS OUT'**   187

CHAPTER 13 **CLARKSON STRIKES OUT**   205

CHAPTER 14 **AROUND THE WORLD WITH
            CLARKSON**   231

CHAPTER 15 **CLARKSON RETAKES THE
            FALKLANDS**   249

CHAPTER 16 **BUST UP**   261

CHAPTER 17 **TOP GEAR ON STEROIDS**   271

CHAPTER 1

A MOTORMOUTH
IS BORN

Jeremy Clarkson is a modern phenomenon. There is no missing him wherever he goes: 6ft 5in tall, in his trademark jeans and mop of unruly hair, these days Clarkson is one of the most recognisable men in the country. And, in this era of vacuous celebrity, he is in many ways a breath of fresh air. Famously acerbic, refusing to bow to authority and not overly concerned about who he might upset, Jeremy has metamorphosed beyond his initial persona as the country's best known motoring broadcaster into a national celebrity who has written books, hosted his own chat show and turned his hand to any number of different crafts. And he's lasted the course, too. It is almost thirty years since Clarkson first appeared on BBC's *Top Gear*, and his popularity is as high as it ever was. There's no chance, for the moment at least, that he's going to go away.

Jeremy has certainly carved out a niche for himself in modern

Britain. Love him or loathe him – and Clarkson is one of those men who divides public opinion – you have to admit that he's made himself known nationwide for his acerbic views, his blunt style of broadcasting, his occasional outrageousness and his sound ability to tell it like it is. He's a bloke's bloke, a man's man and, whatever your views about him, he's simply someone who can't be ignored. But how, exactly, did he get to where he is today?

Clarkson's background is a surprise. He likes to come across as a bit of rough, but the truth is that his was a privileged childhood, with a stable family, good schooling and an exceptionally enterprising mother. On 11 April 1960, Jeremy Charles Robert Clarkson was born to Shirley, a teacher, and Edward, a travelling salesman. It was a comfortable household, although not a rich one, with both parents doing well and able to provide for Jeremy and, a couple of years on, his younger sister Joanna.

The Clarksons were not an inward-looking family. They dealt with everything by having a laugh and that is something that has clearly built Jeremy into the man he is today. His home life was robust, with lots of teasing and with no one taking anything too seriously. It was an utterly secure environment in which to live, with the parents dedicated to the improvement of both themselves and their children. And they were in deadly earnest about that. They might not have been prone to taking life too seriously, but to them their children's education was of paramount importance and, from the very start, they were determined it would be as good an education as it was possible to get and they would work as hard as they needed to in order to attain it.

'From early on, I realised they wanted a private education for my younger sister Jo and I, but they couldn't afford it, so Mum started making bits and bobs on the side,' Clarkson recalled. 'Pouffes and cushions to sell to the neighbours. She was, and still is, a wonderful seamstress.' She was about to put these talents to even greater use.

This was middle-class England on the cusp of the sixties: conservative and non-threatening. The family had a good life and their material comfort, which was not excessive but more than enough for a decent lifestyle, was not the only element of Clarkson's background that shaped him: so, too, was the fact that it was so very secure. Whether or not you agree with his assaults on public consciousness, it actually takes some guts to stand up and take on pretty much everyone. And the only reason Jeremy is able to do so is because he is secure in himself. The knowledge that he was at the centre of his parents' lives gave him the confidence to become such a strong personality.

But the family was soon to become rather more prosperous, all because of a happy opportunity that was shortly to arise. No one had foreseen it when his mother went into business, but it was to have a lasting effect on Jeremy's life. Shirley, who went on to become a magistrate, was an exceptionally able woman: much taken with Paddington, of the Paddington Bear stories, she decided to make little Paddington figures as a Christmas present for Jeremy and his sister Joanna out of fabric purchased from the local market in Burghwallis, near Doncaster, where the family lived.

Unfortunately, she couldn't make the little bear stand up, and so hit upon the idea of putting him in Wellington boots – and so the world-famous Paddington figure was born. For the toys were so popular with her children that Shirley decided to set up a business to make and sell the bears; it was a decision that brought the family some real degree of prosperity and allowed the Clarksons to send Jeremy to a good public school. 'I still remember the day Mum and Dad told us they were jacking in their jobs to set up a toy business,' Jeremy recalled. 'Marine Boy was on the telly and I thought, "Do what the hell you want, Mother, but please shut up!"'

Using her middle name as the name of the company, in 1968 Shirley set up Gabrielle Designs. It was an immediate success. The company grew quickly and, by 1976, demand for the Gabrielle Paddington was so great that production had to move from Shirley's kitchen table to a factory in Adwick Le Street, which became known as the 'Bear Garden'. It was Paddington Bear who funded Clarkson's schooling, holidays and agreeable childhood, and it was Paddington Bear who even gave him some gainful employment, when he worked for the family business for a short time after leaving school.

Edward also began to work for the company, dealing with sales and marketing, while Shirley concentrated on production. So taken was Michael Bond, Paddington's creator, with the little figures that he described them as 'the definitive Paddington'. But that was not the end of Shirley's endeavours: in 1992, by which time her son was already famous, she was granted the licence to manufacture the Classic Winnie the Pooh by The Walt Disney Company. Three years later she sold the company on; three years after that, it shut down.

However, Shirley was not the first member of the family to have displayed an entrepreneurial streak. Jeremy came from a long line of people who were prepared to take any chances offered to them: his mother might have been a very successful businesswoman, but she was only following a family tradition. Many years later, when taking part in a BBC programme about tracing family roots called *Who Do You Think You Are?*, Jeremy discovered that one of his ancestors had manufactured the screw-topped Kilner jar, which was sealed with a rubber ring to preserve food and exported all over the world in the nineteenth and early twentieth century.

For some years the Gabrielle Paddington was the most popular toy in Britain and it is safe to say that the Kilner jar must, decades earlier, have been one of the most popular pieces of kitchenware in the world. Indeed, its creation was part of the whole process by which food could be properly stored and, in the years to come, revolutionise cooking.

Returning to the 1960s, however, all this was both past and in the future. Jeremy's early childhood was a happy one: the family lived in a 400-year-old farmhouse although, by the time he was fourteen and already 6ft tall, Jeremy's head was hitting the ceiling. It was his father who was the family cook, something that might explain the fact that, in later years, Jeremy himself was rather proud of the fact that he too could follow a recipe and, notably, male chefs have never come in for the sort of lambasting he dishes out elsewhere.

'Father cooked, he was a superb cook, was and still is the best cook I ever encountered,' said Jeremy in the 1990s. 'School friends would want to come over and eat and Father was unhappy unless I brought home twenty of them. He spent two days cooking cakes for the birds.' As for his mother: 'Mother rustled up puddings; Mother ate out of a tin.' The fact that Jeremy himself became an extremely competent cook as an adult is one of the many sides to him that the public might be surprised to take on board.

But it is his mother who Jeremy most closely resembles, certainly in temperament. She was as jolly and as straightforward as her son was to become, refusing to take life seriously and never letting anything get her down. 'I was always a bit of a mother's boy,' Clarkson once said. 'I can certainly see a lot of me in her – she's one of those life and soul of the party, bang the furniture, make a joke about anything characters. Even when I was an idiot teenager, I was in awe of her and how she could hold the entire room with one of her stories. Her friends used to call them "Clarkson stories" – they were these elaborately exaggerated anecdotes. I'm sure her friends thought she made them up.'

As for his northern heritage, Clarkson could become a bit irritable about suggestions that his upbringing was some kind of cliché. 'No, we did not have marmalade sandwiches, not at home, but I was partial to halibut and peas, and raspberries and cream – we had a large garden given over to raspberries.' In fact, he tended to associate halibut – with parsley sauce – with his grandfather, who was a doctor and author, and who played a large part in the young Jeremy's life.

He would take the young boy out and about with him and, in later years, would also help his grandson to find gainful employment. Jeremy adored him, although he would never have put it in exactly those words: his was the more gruff type of appreciation that some men find easier to express. 'Built a house by a railway line and everyone said he was mad and then he bought the spur line,' Jeremy mused of his grandfather. It was his way of saying what a wonderful man his grandfather was.

The family would holiday in Padstow in Devon where, of course, Clarkson père was in charge of the cooking, and occasionally in France. The young Jeremy was becoming something of a bon viveur: he once recalled eating langoustines for the first time on one of these holidays and it was something that 'started a love affair with shellfish that persists to this day'. His grandfather would also take him out to smart restaurants, such as the Gingham Kitchen in Doncaster and the 1492 in Marlow. '[It] was very expensive and I ordered strawberries and cream,' Clarkson recalled. 'I was into lobster thermidor. [We] went to the Newton Park Hotel, which smelled of Brussels sprouts cooked for some time. When you reserved a table they asked, "What vegetables?" so that they could start cooking.'

And, even as a child, Jeremy was beginning to stand out. He had a combative streak and was always determined to take on allcomers. As an adult he might not care at all what other people think, but as a child he was still keen to impress, although his way of doing this was by being a rebel. His mother once recalled that, when he was very young, she'd come to the conclusion that as an adult he'd either have no friends or hundreds – and, despite all the feuds he has become embroiled in throughout his adult life, it's fairly safe to say that the latter has turned out to be the case.

Jeremy was, however, not an easy child to bring up. Fairly early on, he lost interest in academic studies, something that caused his long-suffering parents no end of concern. 'I'm sure Jeremy thinks he was a normal child, but my God he was a handful,' Shirley recalled. 'Do you know something? He gave up work when he was eleven. He went from being top of the class to bottom overnight. He told us he didn't think physics or maths were going to be any use to him because he was either going to be Alan Whicker, an astronaut or king – in that order!'

By the time he reached an age to go to senior school, Jeremy's parents were able to send him to Repton School, again, not a place entirely in keeping with his rough-and-ready image. The school had a history of turning out students who would go on to make their mark: old boys include author Roald Dahl, sportsman CB Fry and broadcaster and comedian Graeme Garden. Indeed, given both its academic reputation and its stalwart image, Repton is a somewhat surprising place for Jeremy to have been educated, even though he did turn out to be one of the school's self-confessed rebels.

The history of the school is in some ways a microcosm of the national history of the period and is worth relating, very briefly, here. In 1557, Sir John Port of Etwall died, leaving no male heir and, in consequence, left behind a sum to found a 'Grammar School in Etwalle or Reptone'. There, scholars were to pray on a daily basis for the souls of his parents and for other members of the family.

Two years later, the executors of the will bought, for the princely sum of £13.10s, some land that had once been the site of a twelfth-century Augustinian Priory, and some buildings that had escaped destruction during Henry VIII's Dissolution of the Monasteries. These were the Guest Chamber and Prior's Lodging, Overton's Tower, the Tithe Barn and the Arch, all of which are now part of the school.

In the nineteenth century, the school came into its own. Steuart Adolphus Pears became headmaster in 1854, a post he held for two decades, and it was under his guidance that the school really became one of the great public schools of its day, a position it still holds. Its reputation had declined since it had been founded and Pears found just forty-eight pupils in situ: within three years that number had doubled, staff numbers were increasing and the purchase of land had begun that would make the school a force to be reckoned with.

As in its earliest days, Repton's history in the nineteenth century reflected the wider changes going on in the Victorian world. The industrial revolution brought both progress and wealth in its tracks and the school, like so many of the age, benefited from this. It began to invest in more land, which gave rise to the building of the School Chapel, Orchard House, Latham House, the Mitre and Brook House. Nor was the school merely expanding in size: its reputation was growing, too.

Having become one of the leading headmasters of his day, in 1865 Pears was invited to give evidence to the Schools' Inquiry Commission; he also attended the first Headmasters' Conference in 1869. He prized both academic excellence and sporting prowess and instigated schemes whereby fee-paying students subsidised scholars – this ensured that not only were there places at the school for the less privileged in society, but also that the school was able to attract the very best, whatever their background.

This then was the atmosphere in which the young Jeremy found himself and, it must be said, it was not an entirely happy match. Jeremy was not academic, nor was he particularly concerned about endearing himself to the masters. Even back then he was showing signs of the truculence that was to become his hallmark, something his headmaster recalled only too well. 'It was like being prodded in the chest every day for five years,' he (wearily) said.

Clarkson himself looks back on his schooldays with decidedly mixed views. 'I think I must have been a spoilt brat at home because it was such a shock when I got to school to find that I wasn't king of the hill anymore,' he said, years later. 'I was just another thirteen-year-old fag who was expected to sweep the corridors. And that's why I took this conscious effort to be Jack the Lad, to drink and smoke, so that I could stand out. It was the best decision of my life. Smoking is just fantastic – I love it.'

His attitude towards his schooldays tended to change with his mood, though. On another occasion, he sounded considerably more enthusiastic. 'Looking back, though, those were some of the best days of my life,' he once remarked. 'Boarding school was wonderful and I fitted in perfectly. My only disappointment is that no one ever tried to bugger me. I feel that's a whole important part of growing up that I missed out on.'

But it was certainly different from home. Jeremy realised he had been spoilt in other ways too, not least by the quality of his father's home cooking. 'Steve was the cook,' he recalled of his school days. 'He is now cooking either at a prison or on the *QE2*. I was spoilt by father's cooking, though even if I had been brought up in a Little Chef I would have been disappointed with Repton food. Grease. Water. Chicken: bone, air, skin. They should have been set free. Meat-free birds.'

Food was not his greatest concern back then, however. On another occasion, he recalled what had really occupied his time. 'I was far more interested in the girls than lessons,' he said. 'My parents were in utter despair.' He was developing into the personality he is now but, of course, what works well for a television presenter who won't kowtow to anyone is not good in a truculent schoolboy. It was a difficult situation for all concerned.

Holidays, at least, were a relief. Clarkson was a typical lad about town, hanging out with his mates and chatting up girls and, very many years later, he recalled his attire du choix. It was what he later became famous for wearing, too. 'Choosing the right jeans was critical,' he said. 'One wrong move and all the girls would openly laugh at you in the street. The flare had to come down exactly a quarter of an inch over your platform sole, and then, after I was introduced to The Clash, there had to be no flare at all – just a hole in the knee.

'And under no circumstances could the jean be worn if a crease had been ironed into the front. This would leave an indelible mark: the mark of a man who lives at home with his mummy.'

These preoccupations were not to stay with him for long. Famously careless about his appearance as an adult, this is possibly the only period in his life when Jeremy was seriously concerned about clothes.

Of course, he was also having his formative experiences with girls. Clarkson was never exactly a ladies' man per se, but right from the start he had a healthy interest in the opposite sex and he had quite a number of girlfriends before he finally settled down. Once asked if he'd ever been hurt, he replied, 'Oh, by girlfriends occasionally. Everyone's love life as a teenager is a terrible mess.'

But it was school that was causing the real problem now. Despite the success of the business, Jeremy's parents were having to make a considerable financial sacrifice to send him to the school, something the young Clarkson was well aware of, and yet that did nothing to modify his behaviour. He was difficult in the extreme: constantly challenging the masters, breaking rules, pushing boundaries and seeing what he could get away with. It was perfect training for being a journalist, but at the time his behaviour caused numerous problems. He was awkward, truculent and a nightmare for the masters to have to deal with. And he knew it, too.

He did, however, try to mollify his parents by lurking outside the school to ambush them and provide his own explanation for the latest crisis when they were summoned to see the head.

A MOTORMOUTH IS BORN

'He always had the gift of the gab,' said mum Shirley. 'We used to know how much trouble he was in by how far he was beyond the school gates when we came driving in to see the headmaster yet again. If he was a couple of miles out, it was because he needed quite a lot of time to convince us it was all a horrible misunderstanding.'

At the time he was clearly a challenging pupil. Given the wisdom that years bestow, however, Clarkson did express regret at the way he behaved. 'Mum and Dad must have worked every hour God sent them to get me to Repton,' he said. 'And how did I repay them? I fooled around for five years and got expelled [he was, in fact, asked to leave]. They were bloody livid. And they had every right to be. Don't get me wrong: I knew I was upsetting them, but when you're at boarding school, it's very much out of sight is out of mind. It was only when they came to pick me up at the end of term that the sheer scale of what I was doing to their lives really hit me.'

But back then this was not enough to make him calm down. Clarkson was a rebel, and a conscious one at that. 'At school, there are two ways of getting noticed,' he recalled on another occasion. 'One is to be good at sport, which was out of the question because I was total rubbish at football. The other way is by being Jack the Lad. So I set my stall out. I didn't like beer, but I damn well had to drink it. I had my first cigarette on the moors when we were forced to play soldiers.' It was clear that his actions were ultimately going to bring him into complete conflict with the school, and they did … Clarkson left in somewhat ignominious circumstances a few years later.

'It was a boarding school, so we weren't supposed to go out without permission,' he continued. 'But I used to slide out to see Peter Gabriel and David Bowie at the Derby Assembly Rooms. It was just a collection of minor indiscretions, but it was a public school and you don't need to do that much to annoy them. Had I been at a high school back home in Doncaster, I'd have needed to rape the headmaster's wife and burn the place down to get thrown out.' But, according to Clarkson, at Repton the rules were sacrosanct.

His mother had a slightly different take on events. 'It got to the point where I was being called up to the school every two weeks,' she said. 'The headmaster would say, "Now Mrs Clarkson, has Jeremy even told you what he's done this time?" But he was never into the bad stuff. He never stole things, he never committed a crime; he just spent five years needling the staff and they eventually told me they couldn't put up with it anymore. He was always the one creeping out to have a fag or breaking wind in the two-minute silence. I suppose some kids are like that. You love them dearly, but they're a nuisance.'

Amid all the rebellious behaviour, though, a liking for cars had already taken hold. Jeremy was beginning to discover that he felt very comfortable behind a steering wheel and was keen to develop his new skills as often as he could, something that was encouraged by his much-loved grandfather. And his family's comfortable circumstances were in evidence there, too: it has become part of the Clarkson legend that in 1977 he passed his driving test, at the wheel of his grandfather's 'R' type Bentley.

'I passed my test first time in 1977,' Clarkson proudly recalled.

A MOTORMOUTH IS BORN

'I was so arrogant I even took a pair of scissors along to cut the L-plates off – I saw it as a formality. My first car was a Ford Cortina 1600 E. It was a cool car. It had a wooden dashboard, a picture of Debbie Harry in the middle of the steering wheel and fur on the insides of the doors. I managed to stop short of furry dice; God knows how, because I don't think I suffered from much in the way of taste in those days.'

But his truculent attitude certainly didn't make him any friends among the schoolmasters, and so, perhaps inevitably, Jeremy ultimately left Repton shortly before he was to take his English and History A-levels – something that, in later years, did his reputation no harm at all. Accusations that he's really a posh ex-public schoolboy can always be refuted by the fact that he was, after all, turfed out. It adds to the rebellious reputation and is something that he thoroughly enjoys.

But he did express some regret much later. 'My parents were livid,' he said. 'All that money wasted. It was a hideous time and I don't blame them. There were lots of warnings and my mother would come down and plead for me. I was difficult, disruptive, impatient, cynical and kept asking, "Why?"'

What finally pushed the masters into letting Jeremy go came about when he attempted to sneak off from games and head to the local girls' school. 'I refused to play cricket – it was dull,' he protested. 'There are better things to do when you're seventeen than standing in front of a great yob who's hurling a rock at you, interspersed with enormous periods of standing around suffering hayfever.

'So I thought, "That's it. I'll go to see the birds at Abbots

Bromley." It was 7 miles, 300 yards 2 feet and 4 inches away, to be exact. I know because I traced that route a fair few times. But I wasn't exactly shinning up the drainpipes when I got there. There were twelve day girls at Repton and one of them was my girlfriend, so there was a limit to what I got up to. Still, girls were certainly more interesting than study any day.'

In actual fact this had been brewing for some time. His whole non-conformist approach to life meant that he found it almost impossible to settle down and play by the rules, which meant that, in the atmosphere of a boys' public school, something was bound to give. And that something was the teachers' patience.

'It was for a whole series of misdemeanours,' Jeremy later said of the school's decision to wave goodbye to him, though Repton have never accepted that he was expelled. '[It was] best summed up by the headmaster when he said, "If you'd come up to me on the first day and punched me in the face, I'd have expelled you immediately. And if you'd come up and gone like this" – [Jeremy made a poke in the arm] – "I'd have been mildly irritated. But the thing is, you've been doing that [sharp poke] and that [sharper poke] and that [very sharp poke] for five years. Now get out!" There was no one big thing. I'd worked my way through the rule book, breaking them one by one, but there was no calamitous moment when I was caught in flagrante with the chaplain's daughter. Mostly it was not being there. I was more interested in the local girls' school. "Shall I do my history prep, or shall I go and see Sally Ann?"'

To say that Jeremy's parents were not pleased is to understate the obvious. They were absolutely, utterly incandescent with rage. 'My parents were pretty livid with me,' he recalled. 'They reckoned it was a complete waste of money sending me there. They said they'd worked their fingers to the bone to do it and I was just not taking it seriously. They never forgave me until I was twenty. On the other hand, my sister Joanna was very good at school. She's got lots of qualifications and is now a solicitor. I must have been the black sheep.' He was not entirely blasé about the turn of events, however – 'I was utterly devastated,' he said in later years.

This was certainly not what his parents wanted. Having made such a huge effort to get him into the right school, their son's departure was a blow. Nor did Jeremy himself have any idea what to do next. Any thoughts of being Alan Whicker, an astronaut or the King appeared to have faded, and he had no clear idea what he wanted to do. He had never been particularly set on any realistic career as he was growing up and now, in his late teens, he remained unsure of what to do next. Going to university was out of the question: his early exit from his alma mater had ensured that – not that Clarkson ever wanted to go to university anyway. What he had to do was to find a job.

But no obvious career path presented itself. Jeremy was to spend a little time working in the family business, but he wasn't ready to do so yet and, what's more, it wasn't even an option. Nor was he ready to leave Doncaster: that, too, was still several years away. And so, with the family fretting about what their eldest born and only son would do, it fell to the person to whom Jeremy had looked up for so many years to provide an answer. His grandfather had connections all over the part of the country in which the family lived, and one of these connections was to prove extremely useful. And so, to the surprise of everyone, not least Clarkson himself, the first job of his illustrious career loomed up on the horizon. Jeremy Clarkson was to become a journalist – or, to put it another way, a hack.

CHAPTER 2

THE RISE OF
A LAD

Jeremy Clarkson has been so famous for so long that it is
actually quite hard to associate him with humble begin-
nings. But that, as far as his career was concerned, is exactly how
he started out. As a teenager who had failed to finish school and
who had no qualifications, it didn't exactly appear as if life was
brimming over with opportunities, something Jeremy himself
and his parents were all too aware of. With all that expensive
schooling having gone to waste, even the indomitable Clarkson
was experiencing moments of self-doubt ... and his parents
continued to make their displeasure extremely clear. Back then,
it seemed as if Clarkson was going nowhere fast.

Nor were there any obvious opportunities awaiting him.
While he was still at school Clarkson had no clear idea of what
he wanted to do as a career; after his sudden departure, things
were still no more obvious. There was a real danger of him

drifting along if he didn't manage to find some sort of job – although, saying that, his parents were still so angry with him that they probably wouldn't have allowed that to happen. For a teenager who had been used to breaking the rules and flouting authority, as the reality of his situation set in, Clarkson was suffering a very nasty wake-up call.

Indeed, this period of his life was an unsatisfactory one. His younger sister Joanne was the white sheep of the family: working hard for the future, being a model pupil and doing everything Jeremy hadn't done. The man – or rather, teenager – himself, meanwhile, just didn't have a clue what to do. At this stage in his life, had anyone said that one day Jeremy would become one of this country's most famous faces on television, no one would have believed it. He just seemed to be another teenager with an attitude problem – a reminder, in some ways, of the James Dean character who, when asked what he was rebelling against, replied, 'Whaddya got?'

But something had to be done and a combination of family connections, well-meaning advice and the need to bring in some income – Clarkson's parents were in no mood to subsidise their errant son, although he was still living at home – meant that a decision had to be made, and fast. And so the job in journalism began. It was certainly not something Jeremy had considered when he was growing up: as with so many careers that turn out to be extremely successful, he wandered into it almost by chance. He wandered out of it again, as well, a few years later. It seemed as though his early brush with the profession would not last.

But, back then in the late 1970s, he was prepared to give journalism a go. The *Rotherham Advertiser* was looking for a trainee, Clarkson needed a job and so there it was. And his family history helped there, too. Many years previously, Jeremy's grandfather had delivered the editor's baby during an air raid in the Second World War. The editor was clearly well disposed to the Clarkson family and Jeremy was taken on in his first proper job. And, however hard he may have found it to settle in, at least he wasn't office-bound – indeed, he never has been, at any stage of his career. His role required him to spend a lot of time out and about in the local community and it did not restrict him to a nine-to-five routine. He certainly didn't realise it back then, but Jeremy Clarkson, the former public schoolboy, had landed on his feet.

As it happened, he couldn't have made a better career choice. The best training for a journalist – something that Jeremy still is, albeit one in a different stratosphere – is a small, local paper, where junior staff are taught the rudiments of the trade. They have to learn how to write terse, readable prose and, as anyone who has worked on a local paper will tell you, if you can make a flower show sound exciting, you can write about just about anything with fluency and skill. Forget driving some of the fastest and most exciting cars in the world: Clarkson learned the hard way how to turn very little into a great deal; it is a skill that has stood him in immeasurably good stead as the years have gone by.

Then there are the fundamental principles of how to construct a story: the pyramid principle. This means that all the most crucial information must be contained at the top of the pyramid, within the first three sentences, and that the less important information must be added in as the pyramid widens out. The idea is that the pyramid shape can be sliced sideways from the bottom without harming the construction of the story. Look at anything Clarkson does today, from his newspaper columns to his onscreen reports, and you will see these techniques still apply. He might be utterly individual in what he says and he has indeed developed a unique style of his own, but his way of reporting is still exactly the same as any properly trained hack.

Indeed, so well did he come to learn his trade that it might even be said that being turfed out of Repton had been a blessing in disguise. Had he gone to university (which was unlikely, given how opposed Clarkson was to being an academic teen) or had he even just started work on leaving school in the more conventional way, he might well have embarked on a more mainstream job and never found his true metier. Adversity often brings out the best in a person and, by having to accept a job because there was nothing else on offer, Clarkson inadvertently found himself 'choosing' to do exactly the right thing.

Not that he either realised or appreciated it back then. Jeremy had never planned to become a journalist and to begin with, he didn't think it was much cop. Much later, when asked if he'd decided to become a motoring journalist, he replied, 'No, it never occurred to me until I was expelled or, rather, took voluntary redundancy from school, before my A-levels, for spending too much time at the local girls' school and not doing any work. Then a chap in the village said there was only one profession for those who'd been expelled – journalism – so I got a job on that august organ, the *Rotherham Organiser*.'

Of course, the chap in the village may have been a good deal cannier than he was letting on. The best journalists are iconoclasts: they question everything, never let a story alone until they have got to the bottom of it and refuse point blank to believe any fact at all simply because someone told them so. Truculence and iconoclasm make for the best journalists … and Jeremy had plenty of both. In fact, if you put together a list of the qualities journalists need to get on and compare them with a list of Clarkson's character traits, you would have a near-perfect match. He was made for the profession, and it was created for him.

However, despite the fact that in later years he was to become famous for his ability to communicate, he is adamant that this early foray into reporting wasn't a great success. He was not yet writing about cars and, for a young man keen to make his way in the world, the work he was doing often seemed trivial and dull. 'I was a crap reporter,' he said. 'The worst time was when I got slung out of an inquest for laughing at the evidence, which wasn't funny.' But, although he didn't realise it at the time, he was honing the skills that would one day stand him in such good stead. As for the unfortunate laughing incident, it proved that Clarkson had a very irreverent streak running through him which was one day going to mark him out as one of the strongest personalities on television.

It has sometimes been suggested that this period on the paper was only a very brief part of the young Clarkson's life but, in actual fact, he stuck it out for some time. Three years of training ensued, interspersed with block-release courses at a college in Sheffield. In retrospect, these three years can really be seen as the foundation of his career; they were also years in which Clarkson displayed a certain tenacity, a quality for which he is not always given credit. He gave it a very good shot, continued to ply his trade and learned very quickly as he went on, but he wasn't happy. He was unable to settle into the role and felt he had taken a wrong turn.

Although local newspapers cannot be bettered when it comes to learning the trade of a journalist, they are not, by their very nature, exciting places to work. This was not, after all, Bright Lights, Big City: it was small-town reporting, with a great deal of emphasis on court reporting and local events that would never have made the wider news. Increasingly, Clarkson wanted to be out there, mixing with the best of them, rubbing shoulders with other young people with great careers ahead of them. Instead, he was stuck in a small, local news-gathering organisation: it was not where he saw himself for the next forty years.

He was also still more of a teenager than a grown-up man. The fact that he continued to live at home meant that he had yet to break free and establish himself as an individual: it is hard to be your own man when you're still under the thumb of your parents. He needed to break away from his familiar surroundings, to set himself a whole new list of challenges and begin to look further afield than his home town. Almost

24

everyone has to make this break sooner or later and as long as Clarkson continued to stick with the familiar rather than getting out there in the big wide world, he would never achieve any of his real aims.

And the 1980s were fast approaching. Britain was changing: it was no longer the sleepy, strike-riddled country it had seemed to be for so long. There was an energy in the air that signalled new days were on the horizon, with new opportunities for a young man with everything to play for and nothing to lose. This was a time in which the world was there for the taking, if only you got out and went for it. It was inevitable that something had to give.

And it did. Matters finally came to a head when Jeremy was, of all things, covering a 'ponies and produce' show: 'I had all the Pony Club mothers giving me earache about how, "Well, she shouldn't have been in that class so she shouldn't have won,"' Clarkson recalled. 'I'd been hearing how somebody cheated with his marrow and how someone else's apples had come from Sainsbury's and that they hadn't grown them at all, and then the Pony Club mothers – that's what made me do it. I picked up my typewriter in the press tent at the Wyckersley show and shouted, "Enough!" I thought there must be something better than this out in the big, wide world.'

There was, but he hadn't found it yet. And it was a bold move to make, even if it was an utterly necessary one if he wanted to find any real success. However, there was still no obvious alternative game plan – Jeremy ended up working for the family business – and he was reaching the end of his tether.

A big personality like his was never going to be content in a small world and clearly he felt the need for greater challenges, even if he wasn't yet quite sure what those challenges would be. But he was still young enough – only twenty – to be reckless and get away with it. He had not yet reached an age when it was imperative that he settled into a career.

By now there was something else in his life. Ever since he had passed his driving test, Clarkson's love affair with the motorcar had been growing and he had been indulging it ever since. One of his first cars was a VW Scirocco, a car that many might have thought too small for his 6ft 5in frame. Jeremy agreed that it might well have been, but he loved it nonetheless. 'I was desperately uncomfortable in it and the clutch cable used to saw through the bulkhead and break – but it didn't matter because it was such a lovely car. You'd walk up to it after you'd been shopping and look at it and go, "You're magnificent."' The signs for the future were all there, had anyone just looked for them. Jeremy got a lot more pleasure from his car than from his career, so why not try to combine the two one day?

That Scirocco was going to inspire more outpourings than just praise for its wonderfulness; it was to be the very touchstone of his career. It was while he was searching through various guides to decide what car to buy that the idea first occurred to him that he might return to journalism after all: this time, though, because no one else was doing it well, he would write about cars.

The writing was, to be honest, a bit nerdy and far too technical. It's a wonder no one else realised this at the time, but Clarkson's maverick approach when he finally got going was one of the many reasons he came across as being such a breath of fresh air. It is not stretching it to say that he changed the face of motoring journalism, making it not only lively but also mainstream. He addressed the issues everyone wanted to know about – namely, what the car would do for their image and what was it like to drive – while at the same time making his reporting entertaining. Viewers of BBC's *Top Gear* and the innumerable other programmes Clarkson has been involved with don't just tune in because they want to learn about motoring – they watch because they want to be entertained.

And motor journalism at that time could certainly have done with a change. 'They were all like a trade magazine, this incredibly tedious line-up of facts and details,' Clarkson recalled. 'I wasn't interested in that. I want to know, as I cruised down Doncaster High Street, am I going to look good in this car or not? I didn't give a shit about headroom and bootsills. And it made me start to think: "I wonder if you can write about cars in a different way?"'

You could, but he wasn't going to just yet. Jeremy got his big break relatively young, but he had paid his dues in the run-up to it. His early foray into journalism hadn't been a success and neither was his next scheme. Temporarily, he had returned to the family business to become a travelling salesman selling teddy bears and, although this didn't last for very long, it did herald a major change in the young Clarkson's life. Eager to get on, he decided it was time to swim in the biggest pond in the land and so he moved to London to try out his luck in the Big Smoke.

This was not entirely for career-related reasons — indeed, Clarkson would maintain that back then a career was the last thing on his mind. Other issues played a part, too, not least that he wanted a change. Life in Doncaster was no longer the same: his friends had moved away and the local scene was beginning to pall. He saw his peers starting to do exciting things: they were in jobs and establishing an independent life. Being stuck at home with his parents was not part of the game plan and Jeremy was beginning to realise that he would have to branch out if he was to achieve what he wanted in life.

And so he upped and left, which was one of the best moves he could have made. It was the beginning of a riotous existence, a period in his life that he would look back on very fondly. London in the 1980s was a place brimming with opportunity; there was liveliness in the air and a sense that great adventures lay ahead. An unreconstructed Thatcherite, although he probably would not have described himself as such at the time, this was precisely the kind of atmosphere in which Jeremy thrived. Barriers were breaking down, Britain was changing and the mood of the country was that there was everything to play for. Young, lively and energetic, Clarkson made full use of these early years in London before he settled down: career-wise, he might still have been getting nowhere, but otherwise, London was an awful lot of fun.

And it was certainly a raucous life. Later, when asked what his favourite decade was, he replied, 'The eighties, when Thatcherism was at its best. I was living in Fulham with three other guys. Whenever we ran out of money, there would be another share issue.' This was typically Clarksonian, although it did not tell the full story: Jeremy spent those years both living it up and being broke. An indication of the way in which he and his friends lived was their nickname of the flat, the 'Vomitarium': it was a time of total freedom and for Clarkson, it was the first taste of life on his own … he was enjoying himself to the full.

Evenings were spent at the local pub, the White Horse in Fulham, a lively establishment peopled with those strange creatures who were so prevalent in the 1980s: Sloane Rangers. Jeremy was not exactly a Sloane, but he did have some of the right credentials: a public school education and a bit of family money behind him, even if it wasn't a great deal. There were also indications that he didn't slum it quite as much as the flat's nickname indicated.

Asked once what his biggest regret was, Clarkson replied, 'Having lived in the same block of flats as Lady Diana Spencer and never meeting her. I didn't realise who she was until a media circus arrived one day.' This shines a slightly different light on the bachelor flat: Lady Diana lived in Coleherne Court, which is not by a long shot the home of rundown studenty bedsits. It is a very smart apartment block indeed and rather suggests that Jeremy was living in slightly more style than he would care to admit.

Life, however, was very much a studenty affair. Jeremy's fellow flatmates were friends from his school days and he recalled their existence with a certain amount of glee. 'It was all vomit-stained walls and curry packets – the house from hell,' he said. 'What little money we had went on booze and fags. Women didn't like coming around but, once they did, that was it, because they stuck to the carpet and couldn't get out.' Jeremy had his fair share of girlfriends around this time. He was, in fact, shortly to meet the woman he would marry, but they did not get together as a couple until nearly 1990, which was probably for the best. It meant that Clarkson could play the field and get it all out of his system before he was ready to wed.

And he had lots of fun – and otherwise – here, too. He moved in a circle in which everyone was young and willing to play as hard as they worked (actually, in Clarkson's case, he frequently claimed he did hardly any work at all) and so there were plenty of young women happy to go out on dates. Jeremy had a healthy interest in women and enjoyed this period of his life enormously, although not everything always went according to plan. In later years, he would talk about his dating experiences: it certainly wasn't all wine and roses.

There was a blind date when, he said, rather ungallantly, 'She turned out to be a walrus – I talked to the carpet all night.' And there was one girl – 'I can't tell you about her here, but I'd never go out with anyone from Hampshire again.' The only person he ever chucked was, 'A drug addict. When I found out I went into hiding. Otherwise I've always been the one who was dumped.'

And one of those occasions was rather painful, as could be gained from another remark he once made. Asked what the worst way he'd been dumped had been, Jeremy replied, 'The worst way anyone can dump you is by going off with your best friend. I won't comment further.' But he was young, resilient and bounced back almost immediately. Clarkson has actually been very fortunate in his private life: apart from these early experiences, he married at what is these days a young age – thirty-five – and was lucky enough to have a relationship that was very content.

And, meanwhile, there was work. It is hard to imagine Clarkson as a teddy bear salesman, but he made an attempt at it for a while. His parents, after all, had done an enormous amount for him: as well as putting him through Repton, they were now actually employing him and that, in turn, gave him the chance to explore life in the capital while he worked out what he wanted to do next. It was a job, it funded his social life, it was actually helping the family and at least it gave him a short-term aim in life. And, again, there didn't seem to be a great many other options. Clarkson was disinclined to look for a job on another paper but, being entirely without qualifications, he was hard-pressed to know what else to do.

But if truth be told, his heart didn't really seem to be in his new job. At that time life was about socialising, not careers, and his job was, in many ways, an adjunct to what he really wanted to do, which was to party. 'I was supposed to tour the country selling them [the bears], but they sold themselves, so I fooled around, living in the London Vomitarium,' Jeremy said. 'Very laddish – well, who isn't in their early twenties? It was get home, be sick, eat Disprin and nurse a hangover until it was time for the pub again.' The message was clear: he wasn't taking anything seriously, least of all what he would do in the longer term.

On another occasion, however, he was less frivolous about

what life was like back then and, despite the fact that he was relishing his new world, it clearly wasn't all plain sailing. It was hard work and sometimes seemed as if there was little reward. 'I'd drive all the way to Cwmbran or Pontefract, where the usually horrid proprietor of a gift shop would listen to my spiel and then say, "no thanks" and I'd drive back to London,' he recalled recently. It was not his finest hour. Being a salesman also means having to please the customer, rather than the other way around: a man like Jeremy would not always have relished having to stay on the right side of the person with whom he was dealing. It didn't suit his personality at all.

But what should he do? He didn't want to continue working for his parents' business, he knew that, but neither did he want to return to local newspapers. And so he pondered on what was the best course to take, what he would be happy doing, how he wanted to live – until an idea that had been brewing for some time began to take hold. He might not have enjoyed his stint on the paper, but it had proved one thing to him: he could definitely write. And then there was his great interest: cars.

The more Jeremy knew about them, the more he liked them, and he began to wonder if he could do something with that liking in the professional sphere. He had already noted how bad a great deal of motoring journalism was, and he felt it seemed to be written for the motor trade itself, rather than for the consumer. He thought that there was a gap in the market, a gap that, just possibly, he might be able to fill.

And why not? This was a time of opportunity and, given that he was still so young, Clarkson had relatively little to lose.

It would be a way forward, a way of carving out a name for himself while doing something he actually enjoyed. The trick of a good career is to make your hobby your job, which means that you will always be passionately interested in what you're doing, and Clarkson was about to do just that.

But he was insistent that this was not the culmination of a long-held dream. Quite the opposite, in fact: it was only as an adult that he really began to develop a passion for cars. 'As a child I wasn't remotely interested in them, in fact I didn't take much notice until I wanted to buy one and found that all the magazines were rubbish,' he said. 'They didn't tell you what to buy and what to avoid. I have been very passionate about them ever since, which is why I get frustrated by rubbish, designed by people who don't care.'

In retrospect, it was the obvious course to take, but it was a bold move at the time, for it entailed leaving the safety of the family firm and launching out into a new business by himself. But in the 1980s the entrepreneurial spirit was going strong, and Jeremy was only twenty-four. There was one risk: if the venture didn't succeed, it would be yet another career path that hadn't quite worked out for him. However, he was determined and willing to take a risk and so, in 1984, the Motoring Press Agency was born.

To say that it took off immediately would be to overstate the case. To begin with, it was a long, hard grind. Clarkson had practically no experience of motoring journalism and virtually no contacts anywhere, so he had to get going from scratch. But he worked hard and began syndicating a motoring column, which again gave him the chance to learn his trade before his career really took off.

The man himself was typically self-deprecating about it: 'Only two papers took it, which required twenty minutes of writing on a Thursday and gave me the rest of the week to sit in the pub, go to the bookies and watch *Danger Mouse* on television,' he said. 'I ran the business with a friend and, after three years, we'd earned only £4,000 between us and had massive overdrafts, but we were invited to loads of fantastic car launches.' Back then, that in itself was a reason for joy. It was different from anything Clarkson had experienced before: for a start, he was actually enjoying what he was doing. That, if nothing else, made a break with the past.

And anyway, who cared whether the work was steady and the income less than lavish? This was the 1980s, when life was one big party. 'It was a question of fumbling around in the morning, pretending to work, then meeting the rest of Thatcher's children in the pub,' said Clarkson. 'They were all self-employed, too. I have no regrets about the eighties – they were brilliant.' They were certainly made for people like him.

But his style back then was very different from what it is now. The Clarkson persona took years to develop and even after he started presenting *Top Gear*, he was much, much softer than he is now. His position as a freelance hack on the very fringes of the motor trade was a very precarious one and, at that stage, he didn't want to upset anyone. Looking back, Clarkson himself mocked his early style: 'The camshaft does this and it does this many miles to the gallon, and the coat hook's in the wrong place. It's all lovely and can I come to your next press launch, please? – never criticising in case I got put on their blacklist,' he said.

And, for some time at least, it would appear that his new writing career was going nowhere fast. On another occasion, Clarkson related how he would spend an hour writing his column on Tuesday mornings, throw away his bank statement telling him he'd got an overdraft ('Well, if you've got an overdraft, you've got an overdraft') and spend much of the rest of the day having a flutter on the horses, playing Scrabble and watching *Danger Mouse* every afternoon. *Danger Mouse* was clearly a big element in his life back then.

But, in 1989, all that was to change. Jeremy was invited to yet another car launch and, on this occasion, it was the seating arrangements at the launch that worked in his favour. He fell into conversation with the person he was sitting next to and, in no time at all, found he was making him laugh – irreverence was a part of his personality from the start. This individual was rather taken with the brash, opinionated young northerner with a good sense of humour, to such an extent that he began to wonder if the two of them could do business together. As it turned out, they could. For the person sitting next to Jeremy was not just any old motoring journalist: he was the producer of *Top Gear*.

CHAPTER 3

MARRIAGE & MOTORS

At first Clarkson could not quite believe what was happening. There he was, bumming around London, making just enough money to get by on writing about cars and having a fantastic time in the process, and now someone, out of the blue, was offering him the opportunity of a lifetime. The producer from the car launch thought he had spotted some real potential and, shortly afterwards, Clarkson was invited to do a screen test. 'I thought it was a complete joke,' said Jeremy. 'I didn't even prepare for it.'

At the time, *Top Gear* was a little-watched, if well-respected, magazine programme, not the entertainment show we know today. Until that day the thought of a career in television had never even occurred to Clarkson. Writing about cars was all very well, but appearing on television and talking about them? No one was more astonished by the turn of events than Clarkson himself, and he was even more flabbergasted when he got the result of the test. He had come across well on the screen and the producers invited him to start work on the show.

With hindsight, of course, it's clear that Jeremy is a natural on television. For a start, he has a very striking appearance: tall, with that startling mass of curly hair, which may be a little more under control these days but remains as striking as ever. His face came across well, too. Clarkson has a long face, which gives him the vague look of an Eeyore, but it is one that is very well suited to the camera. In short, there would be no problems with the way he looked.

And then, even more importantly, was the way he sounded. Although he had never done any training for television, Clarkson's voice was perfect: deep, individual and clear. In addition, he was opinionated and had the ability to make people laugh. It would take a while before Jeremy really got into his stride as far as stirring up rows was concerned – to begin with he was as polite as anyone who was keen to make a good impression – but even then there was a hint of irreverence. He had a certain way with words; a way that made people laugh. And he was also very good at the studied pause, at drawing the sentence out to create tension and putting emphasis on particular words to make a point. All in all, he had exactly the qualities that were needed.

And so he started to appear on the show. It was by no means an overnight success, however. Clarkson joined a rota of presenters and did not immediately start by being rude about the car he was reviewing or even comparing it to a quail's egg in Julia Roberts' belly button: in contrast, he was pretty straightforward in the way he talked. And a good deal of this was because the producers of *Top Gear* did not want to cause controversy; they just thought their presenters should get on and talk knowledgeably about cars.

But this was not an approach their soon-to-be star presenter agreed with. 'The show was crap at that time,' Jeremy said. 'I've got no idea what makes cars work. If somebody told me to change the plugs, I'd be looking in the boot. I'm interested in what cars say about you, not what makes 'em work.' This was exactly the attitude Clarkson took when it came to writing about cars, but for now he was the new boy, so he kept his head down and got on with his work.

By the time he started to appear on television, Jeremy had already met the woman who would become one of the most important people in his life — indeed, he had known her for the best part of a decade. Their initial meeting came about because, soon after he moved to London, he was put in charge of organising a treasure hunt: it was in the course of doing this, when both were with groups of people in the same place, that he met Frances Catherine Cain, known always to her friends as Francie. It was not a particularly auspicious occasion: neither of them was particularly taken with the other.

At the time the two couldn't have been more different: Jeremy was living in a shabby house with three mates and earning nothing; Francie, meanwhile, was a power-suited executive who worked as a redundancy counsellor, with her own flat and a Golf GTI — the epitome of yuppie, dog-eat-dog motoring. 'We had mutual friends and ended up in the same restaurant one night,' Francie recalled. 'We had an argument about whether it was better to be a woman or a man.' It would come as no surprise to many that Clarkson's favoured method of wooing would be to involve his wife-to-be in a heated debate.

But Jeremy wasn't wooing Francie back then. It certainly wasn't love at first sight, although they mixed in the same circles for nearly ten years before they started dating. Indeed, they didn't really take to each other at first. 'Jeremy terrified me,' Francie recalled. 'At the treasure hunt, he was very bossy and noisy. He was terribly loud and very big – he's more than a foot taller than me. If a group of us went to a restaurant, I'd always be thinking, "Please don't let the empty seat be next to Jeremy Clarkson. He's frightening."'

Nor was Jeremy particularly smitten. 'And I'd be thinking, "Oh, there's Francie, a career girl wearing a suit and too much red lipstick,"' he said. '"Please don't let her sit next to me – I'll have to be all grown up."' Indeed, he said on another occasion, 'All my friends were bums, just like me, and while she was going to the opera, I was sitting in the pub.' In many ways, it's surprising they ever got together at all: Francie appeared to be career-driven, Jeremy anything but, and there were no real feelings of sympathy between either of them either way.

This changed, however, when it emerged that Francie was really one of the lads, too. Clarkson was suddenly able to relax in her company and appreciate that she could be as juvenile as his male friends. 'Francie suddenly said she wished she was a man because it must be so much easier to get laid,' said Jeremy nostalgically. 'And because men can pee off the side of a boat,' Francie chipped in. 'I'd once been in Sydney Harbour drinking a lot of beer with some boys and then discovered the loo on the boat didn't work. That didn't present any problem to the blokes – most unfair.' Jeremy continued: 'At the end of the meal, I remember thinking, "She's not only successful and pretty, and generously breasted, she's good fun too."' They finally became a couple in 1990.

And, now finally together, the relationship became serious very quickly, with Jeremy showing a romantic streak of the sort that his detractors would never have guessed. 'Although we never discussed it, I think that both of us must have worried that we didn't want to jeopardise our friendship by getting involved,' said Francie. 'But one night in 1990, we both had a little too much to drink and Jeremy stayed over. I was going on holiday the next day and he said that he wished I wasn't going. I said that I wished he could come with me to Greece. When I got to Heathrow that afternoon, there he was, waiting at the check-in desk.

'We had a wonderful week, then Jeremy had to come home. He missed my birthday, so when he came to pick me up from the airport, he was loaded down with presents. He's very romantic. Our relationship became very close, very quickly. I knew he was the man for me; he made me laugh. In some ways we're really different, but we have a similar sense of humour and we're both very, very competitive.'

This was the start, as it were, of the domestication of Jeremy and the period in which he grew up. He had been living in convivial squalor for years now, but he was growing up and time was moving on. The 1980s, with all its excitement, was giving way to the slightly quieter 1990s and, as Jeremy and his friends entered their thirties, everyone was beginning to settle down. After all, living like a student is one thing as a very young man, but Clarkson was getting to an age where if he continued to live in such a way, it would have been a bit tragic. It was time for another change.

And Francie was just the woman to bring it about: she immediately set about introducing some order into his life. 'He didn't do a lot of washing before I met him,' said Francie. 'Didn't do a lot of eating, either. The first things I bought him were a roll of loo paper and a tin of Complan.' Not that Francie herself had planned on the relationship becoming more serious. 'I was very committed to my career,' she said. 'I never thought I'd get married and have children – I was a hard-living single girl.'

Of course, by now Jeremy had started to appear regularly on *Top Gear*, another development that was going to take him from being just another motoring hack to one of the most successful broadcasters in the country. But he was still at the very beginning of his career and he still had the same penniless lifestyle he had had before he got together with Francie, which meant that, when he moved in with her, as he did shortly afterwards, she was very much the main earner. Clarkson was not, at that point, a very good proposition at all.

'Francie was keeping me,' Jeremy recalled. 'We were living in her flat and I was up to my ears in debt. I didn't dare tell her how bad my finances were and how I was so hideously overdrawn. It wasn't until a new production team came into the programme in 1992 and told me to go for it and say what I believed, that my career really changed. But I'm very happy that we met when I was penniless and that we were able to grow together and share the pleasures of it. What we've done, we've achieved together. We're very much a team. I certainly couldn't do this on my own. But then she's just as interested in making it work as I am.'

In time, Francie was to become Jeremy's manager, which gave her the chance to look after her family and yet still stay close to her husband's career. Back then, though, marriage was not the obvious next step – for Francie, at least. It was certainly beginning to seem like a good idea to Jeremy, not least because he wanted children, and so he made the proposal a memorable occasion: asked once what the most romantic gesture he'd ever made was, Clarkson replied, 'Proposing to my wife in San Francisco on a trolley car. I had the time and place all planned, since we both like the city.' Francie said yes.

The couple married in Fulham in 1993 and even there Jeremy couldn't resist a laddish moment, although with an extremely stylish twist. 'I was driven to the wedding in a London taxi because I wanted a few beers,' he said. 'A Dodge Viper took us from the church to the reception.' That was it: the deal was done. Lad-about-town Jeremy Clarkson was now really entering the world of grown-ups: he was a married man.

He was an increasingly successful one too. His early years on *Top Gear* may not have been particularly notable but, by 1992,

Jeremy was really beginning to establish a style that was his own. It was making him stand out and the producers were delighted. For the first time in its history, *Top Gear* was becoming must-see television. But not everyone was pleased.

Jeremy had now started to be brutal about some of the cars he was reporting on, so much so that car manufacturers began to kick up a storm. After announcing that Toyota Corollas were one of the worst cars ever made and that they had been designed like a washing machine, Toyota banned him from test driving its cars, a move emulated by Vauxhall after he savaged the Vectra (something he was to do again years later). 'Both companies have almost forgiven me now,' he said in 1995. They might have done, but that didn't stop him from laying into as many other cars as he could think of.

'Then I was fortunate enough to get on *Top Gear* and say what I liked,' he said of his move from writing a motoring column to fronting a television programme. 'There have been so many crap cars, but the FSA Polinez shines as a beacon of awfulness. It was just ghastly. Poor old Poles in the middle of the Communist thing; there wasn't much in the way of competition. All it could do was physically move; it didn't steer or stop. But it would move. It would get you to wherever you were going, provided it was in a straight line away from you.'

The motor industry was shocked – but the viewers weren't. They loved it. Clarkson began to stand out from the other presenters because of the fact that he was often colossally rude. But the ruder he got, the more the viewers tuned in. *Top Gear* had always had low ratings: as Jeremy increasingly exercised a rather deft wit alongside his willingness to upset, more and more people began to tune in. People began talking about Clarkson, this immensely tall television presenter, who was not afraid to take on the giants of the car industry. They loved it, and they wanted more. And so, of course, seeing what was happening to the ratings, the producers encouraged Jeremy to be as beastly as he liked. He duly obliged.

Life was beginning to change in other ways too. Clarkson was becoming a celebrity. People were recognising him in the street. He was getting commissioned to other programmes as well as *Top Gear*, although at that stage everything he did was in some way related to the motor industry, and this paid. Jeremy was beginning to earn some proper money for the first time: Francie had been told years earlier about her husband's dreadful financial situation, but now that, too, was thankfully a thing of the past. They were beginning to live in some style, because with Francie also still working, they had quite an income between them. Both of them liked the good life and they were happy to live it to the full.

And as they became wealthier, their family began to grow, too. Their first daughter, Emily, was born in July 1994. Jeremy, naturally, was abroad, filming *Motorworld* in Iceland, and so could not be present at the event. He was, however, utterly delighted and celebrated in his own inimitable way. 'She rang when I was on a glacier and said, "Thank you very much, I've just driven myself to hospital!"' Jeremy recalled some months after the event. 'I got Emily a baby walker after Christmas, her first set of wheels.'

By now living in a house in Battersea in London, Jeremy was increasingly in demand. He once described a typical day as getting out of bed by six, smoking a host of cigarettes while the coffee was on the boil and leaving the house by seven to avoid the traffic. This meant that he also, inadvertently, avoided Emily: 'I like to be out of the house, not because I don't like her, but because if you leave it any later the traffic is just too awful,' he explained. He also went on to profess a hatred of the countryside, an attitude that he was later to change. Days when he was not filming, according to him, were spent smoking and writing in the basement conversion, a scene he merrily enhanced by explaining how his cigarettes would sometimes set the accumulated faxes on fire.

But despite the abrasiveness, Jeremy was also beginning to display an odd sort of calm. That can certainly be the only explanation for him managing to insult Noel Edmonds and simultaneously getting him involved in his work. 'We were filming in a Ford GT40 and we found out that I was 9 inches too tall to get into it,' Clarkson recalled. 'So I rang Noel Edmonds and said, "You're a short-arse, so can you do this for us?" And he did.'

He was also extremely self-deprecating. There is no better way of deflecting personal criticism than by getting in there first yourself, and Jeremy certainly managed that. Take his description of himself: 'My stomach is the size of a Spacehopper, I weigh 16 stone and my teeth are yellow from smoking far too much,' he announced. It took the wind out of his detractors' sails before they even had the chance to utter a word.

And those detractors were beginning to gather. Anyone who has a strong personality and isn't afraid to speak their mind will attract attention, and not all of it positive. Not only was Jeremy becoming famous in some quarters, he was becoming infamous as well. Right from the start, environmental groups were never going to make up a big part of his fan base for obvious reasons, but his point-blank refusal to concede that any of them had so much as an iota of a point about anything merely served to enrage them all the more. Car manufacturers themselves were also none too thrilled by a lot of the banter (and it takes quite some personality to get environmentalists and motor manufacturers up in arms about the same thing) and Clarkson's many and varied prejudices were also beginning to make themselves felt.

But why should Jeremy care about any of that? His television bosses were thrilled by the impact he was having on *Top Gear*, while the man himself was rather enjoying the fact that he was increasingly becoming a focal point for controversy. It was a trait that was to grow, and grow.

CHAPTER 4

STRAIGHT TALKING

Right from the start, Jeremy had proved himself capable of causing controversy and provoking a sometimes irate if not over-the-top response to his forthright style and, by the mid-1990s, he had established himself as one of the nation's leading controversialists. His range extended far beyond the car market: he could chat about a huge variety of topics and was strongly opinionated about most of them too.

And there were already signs that his career was going to be a lot bigger than that of most television presenters: although he'd only been on television for a few years, he was already becoming a household name. He seemed to be everywhere: not only on television, but in all the papers and magazines, too. Young men, in particular, loved him: his favourite subject – cars – was theirs too, which meant they were fans from the off. On top of that, they loved his macho style of reporting, his fearlessness and his refusal to countenance any form of political correctness. If truth be told, Clarkson was the man his fans wanted to be.

Nevertheless, he was already getting his fair share of detractors, too. Given that he started having a go at various interest groups, nationalities and who knows what right from the start of his career, it is hardly surprising that not everyone was a mad keen Clarkson fan. But, love him or loathe him, you couldn't ignore him, and for that reason, one group of his fans – his BBC employers – simply adored him. Every time Jeremy got some publicity, his television programmes did too.

And he showed that not only could he dish it out, he could also take it. On one occasion, he received a letter from a doctor after saying that motorway speed limits should be raised to 130mph. Jeremy related: 'He said he was looking forward to my daughter being killed in a road accident. Nice chap … My serious point was that it isn't speed that kills, otherwise Concorde would be the most dangerous form of travel – and to date the number of people killed on Concorde is a big fat zero. [This was, of course, before the tragic Concorde crash over the Parisian suburb of Gonesse in July 2000, which led to the plane being decommissioned – indeed, Jeremy was to be one of the passengers on its last flight.] The problem is that people aren't concentrating because driving is too easy at a low speed. Go faster and they'd concentrate more.'

Jeremy would go on to celebrate the invention of the jet engine in his 2004 BBC series *Inventions That Changed The World*, offering his own opinionated take on the benefits of the jet, as well as the computer, the television and the gun. 'My go-faster comments were tongue in cheek – but, apparently, now I am going to get a letter from an MP. Oh no! I'm quaking … I don't have much respect for MPs.'

Of course he didn't. Members of Parliament, after all, represent authority figures and Clarkson was building his career on standing up to them. It was the truculent schoolboy inside him coming out again but this time round, the qualities that made him so difficult as a teenager were standing in his favour. Truculence, obstinacy, a refusal to kowtow to anyone, allied with a grown man's authority, were the perfect traits to make him stand out. And while a troublesome teenage boy is simply irritating, a troublesome grown man, who is willing to prick some of the most over-inflated egos in the land is something else entirely. Clarkson was still causing trouble, but now it was trouble worth causing.

He was loving it. Sometimes it seemed as though every time he opened his mouth he caused a row, but that, of course, was exactly what Jeremy wanted. He had been a truculent little schoolboy and now he was a truculent adult enjoying nothing more than to upset people, pricking pomposity and getting a rise out of the self-proclaimed great and good. And he was passionate about his job, too. Jeremy might have drawn a lot of attention to himself by taking on anyone and everyone, but he loved cars and saw his role both as a mission to explain and to entertain.

And he countered the motor industry's many complaints about him with an admirable argument: he was there to look after the interests of the car buyer, not the car manufacturer. He was not there to sell their cars: he was there to decide whether their cars were worth buying. It is amazing, in some ways, that anyone would have thought otherwise, but the fact is that Clarkson was there to stand up for the little man, the car buyer, the consumer on the street. Of course, he would frequently go too far, describing his dislikes in such extreme terms that it was difficult to escape the conclusion that he was simply doing it for dramatic effect, rather than simply to make his point. But if it engaged the viewers' interest, then what was the problem? No one could accuse Clarkson of failing to get his message across.

And no one was more aware of the full nature of his role than the great man himself. 'My job is to entertain people on telly,' he said. 'I use cars as a prop, and if some car manufacturers don't like what I'm doing, tough. My job isn't to prop up the car industry. A car has to have a soul. The Japanese can fulfil the dictionary definition of a car, but they're as dull as dishwater. A car is not just a means of moving you around; it's something you can develop a relationship with. A good car talks to you. You should actually enjoy washing a Jaguar. I think people should buy British if they possibly can.' Of course, in later years, Jeremy was to be accused of having far too much influence over the motor industry, but his creed has always been quite simple: if it's good, buy it. If it isn't, don't.

And anyway, he always point blank denied that his opinions had any real force in the marketplace at all. 'When the K-registered Escort came out in '92, I rubbished it on TV; I just annihilated it, I said it was a dog,' he said. 'And it went on to be Britain's best-selling car. And then with the Renault A610, I said this is fabulous, you should all have one, and that year Renault sold six. So you see, nobody takes the slightest bit of notice.'

Renault, incidentally, was one of the many car companies that Jeremy managed to upset along the way, something he wore as a badge of pride. 'I don't write for car manufacturers,' he said. 'My favourite was Renault, who I once upset, not by something I said, but by breaking an embargo, which is something I do as a matter of course. And they were livid. Renault in France told Renault in Britain to pull all their advertising off the BBC. And, of course, Renault in England had to say, "Sorry, we can't really do that on account of there being none."'

But the audience loved it. For every person who got upset by Jeremy's abrasive manner, there were at least two people who didn't. As a result, his popularity soared. Some saw him saying things they wouldn't dare to say; others merely enjoyed the spectacle of seeing someone who wasn't afraid to cause a fuss. Jeremy knew that, and played on it, too. He was as aware as anyone of his image and whether or not it worked in his favour: on the whole, of course, it did.

'I'm not bothered by the hate mail,' he said. 'If you have an opinion, other people will disagree with it. The alternative is to be grey and brainless and host a game show. I try to maintain a 51 per cent rule – never annoy more than 49 per cent of people at any one time.' But, he was asked, did he ever mind upsetting people? 'Oh, of course,' said Clarkson blithely. 'Sometimes you think, "Oh dear, I've hurt someone and that's awful." But then you have a drink and forget about it.'

His popularity was demonstrated in *Top Gear*'s viewing

figures. Pre-Jeremy, the show had a rather earnest air about it; after his arrival, it was frequently as uproarious as the man himself. The ratings rocketed: in the six or so years since he'd been doing the programme, a further 6–7 million viewers were tuning in. As long as that continued to be the case, of course, Jeremy could get away with an awful lot – and he knew it. He understood what made the programme popular, too: the chance for the vast majority of men who would never get to go anywhere near a really amazing car to feel that they were involved in the whole set-up, too.

'You might say we lean a little too much towards Aston Martins and Ferraris and TVRs, but then *Top Gear's* your one opportunity to find out what it's like to be inside one of those things going very, very fast,' he said. 'That, and the fact that there's rubbish on the other sides.'

And still he continued in his straight-talking manner, not only when it came to cars but also about car drivers, too. This is Jeremy's view of people who drive Nissans: 'They can't park, don't understand roundabouts and are not averse, once in a while, to driving the wrong way down a motorway.' When one interviewer went to visit him and found Clarkson driving, of all things, a Nissan Primera – which turned out to be on loan for testing purposes – Jeremy was quick with a verdict: 'The most ordinary, depressingly dull corporate junk, although actually there's an inherent niceness about its steering and its responses.'

And he played up the image of a tough old soul in every area of his life. 'My wife Francie is very caring, very liberal, and I'm not, which makes dinner times very interesting,' he explained.

'I'll be exploding with rage because some young thug has been sent off to the Red Sea for nicking a car, and she's explaining he had a deprived childhood.' There was, though, whether he admitted it or not, a decidedly more sympathetic side to Clarkson when it came to people less privileged than himself. 'If I was a fourteen-year-old kid brought up on a council estate in Doncaster and stood no chance of getting a job, then yeah, I'd nick cars,' he said. 'I'd be reversing into Dixons every night.'

This caused the usual uproar, but it was not a facetious remark. Clarkson himself had come from a privileged background in Doncaster and was, a little unusually for him it must be said, displaying some sympathy for those people who had not had his opportunities or luck. It displayed a depth to his character that was not usually on view. He was as aware as anyone else of the growing social problems in Britain – he was, after all, a father – and the gulf that was developing between the haves and the have-nots. And while he would never be mistaken for a bleeding-heart liberal, neither was he as unfeeling a man as many liked to make out. There was a complexity even at the heart of Clarkson, one of the most straightforward men in society today.

He could never, however, understand environmentalists and had a strong suspicion that they were merely troublemakers. 'I'd like to take photos of every demo, the M11, Brightlingsea, this lot outside Windsor Castle, and then see how many are the same,' he said. 'They're just professional demonstrators. I'd like to announce we were pulling down the veal farms just to confuse them.'

It went without saying that Jeremy was not impressed with the attempts at environmentally friendly cars. The Sinclair C5 came in for particular scorn. Asked if he'd ever use it, Jeremy replied, 'Only as an outside toilet. It was never going to work. Sitting in a slipper with a 92-tonne truck bearing down on you. Don't tell me about pollution. When you charge your electric car, the electricity in your house is coming from a power station – hardly environmentally friendly.'

Indeed, Jeremy was becoming increasingly defiant about his non-PC lifestyle. If the health lobby was for it, he was against it, and he was having no truck with the do-gooders who wanted to influence his lifestyle. Nor was he going to smarten up his image, as everyone was telling him to. 'I'm not bothered what I look like,' he said. 'I don't own a suit; I wear jeans, I have one tie. These boots have got holes in them. I'm about 16 stone, I'm fat and happy. I like chocolate, so I eat it. I like beer, I drink it.'

Nor did these attitudes just extend to the UK: Jeremy was perfectly happy to export his lifestyle with him. 'In Santa Barbara, the lampposts are covered with things you're not allowed to do,' he said. 'No smoking, no smiling, no laughing, no skateboarding, no surfing, no eating, no drinking – you can't do anything! I like going to California and smoking. I'm the guy on the plane asking who smokes and, if it's a majority, asking why we can't light up. I smoke forty a day and pay a huge amount to government coffers. I'll die before I'm old and incontinent, saving the NHS fortunes. I won't cost a penny in pensions; I'll be long gone. I can't stand nanny state stuff, or this American thing when half the world's a lawyer. Trip on a paving stone and you get half a million quid. It's your own fault – watch where you're going!'

Of course, this kind of attitude attracted enemies and even then, more than a decade ago, Jeremy was managing to cause full-scale upset because of the blatant non-PC nature of his remarks. 'You should never buy French or Spanish cars because the Frogs are our oldest enemies and the Spaniards murder bulls and can't cook,' he once said.

France and Spain could take care of themselves, of course, but about this time Jeremy started to cause problems with large parts of England, too. To this day, Clarkson battles against the county of Norfolk – and vice versa – but it all started back in 1995 when he remarked that, 'Norfolk people are so interbred they don't know the difference between a Ferguson tractor and a Ford Capri.' This did not go down well and nor did Jeremy expect it to. Battle promptly commenced.

It was this, in fact, that led to the formation of a club for Jeremy-haters, which made its debut at the 1995 Motor Show. Clarkson was blithely unconcerned. 'In a way, it's a real honour,' he remarked. 'I think almost the whole motor industry belongs to it now.' And as for the feud with Norfolk, he was utterly unrepentant, explaining that he formed his view after an attendant at a Norfolk petrol station didn't know what to do with Clarkson's credit card and ended up putting it in the till. 'I thought he was having me on,' said Jeremy. 'How can you not know what to do with a credit card?'

But even Jeremy's friends were not exempt from his take-no-prisoners style. In the Clarkson household, red meat was the order of the day: both in conversation and on the table itself. And woe betide anyone who thought otherwise – not least anyone who didn't eat red meat. 'They roll up and announce, "I'm a vegetarian,"' sniffed Clarkson. 'They're really saying, "Cook me something special." If we've got veggies coming round, we'll make stew and mashed potato. When they say, "We'll just have the veg," they get a plate of mash. If you want to be a veggie, fine, eat yer lettuce leaves at home, have a nice time. But don't come to my house and expect me to make you a nut cutlet, 'cos you'll be out of luck.'

At the same time, he remained full of surprises. If there was one man in the world you would not have thought of as a 'new man', it was Clarkson but, to some people's amazement, he could actually cook, a talent he had clearly inherited from his own father. 'Only a complete illiterate buffoon couldn't follow a recipe,' he announced. But anyone who thought he was mellowing should think again: 'Food is really just a prelude for smoking – a bit like sex,' he explained. 'You have to go through the whole procedure just so you'll enjoy a fag more than you would if you hadn't done it.'

It was vintage Clarkson, and despite all the outrage, his most notable feature was that he continued to amuse. One newspaper got him to go shopping and drew him out on the subject of the shop's trolleys' steering capability: 'They go exactly where you want them to because they have proper rotating wheels,' he explained. He was equally entertaining on the contents of the trolley, as he piled Budweiser into it: 'It's the only thing the Americans can do better than us. They make good cars but great beer. I can't stand all that real-ale stuff – Old Buttleton's Bottom or Old Man's Underpants, the stuff with twigs in it and old soil.'

As his popularity grew, so too did the amount of time he spent on television. By now he wasn't just presenting *Top Gear*: other commissions were flooding in thick and fast as well. In 1996, he made *Jeremy Clarkson's Motorworld*, a BBC Two programme with a book tie-in, which gave him the chance to visit twelve different countries and subject them to Clarkson-style scrutiny. It was another ratings hit.

One of the many reasons for Jeremy's increasing success was that his public persona also chimed in with the philosophy of laddism. The mid-1990s were the heyday of lads' magazines, lads' telly and a laddish culture that gave many men back their feelings of masculinity, while mixing it all in with a lot of fairly childish fun. Chris Evans was at the height of his popularity and was the biggest lad of them all. The original lads' magazine, *Loaded*, was still going strong. BBC's *Men Behaving Badly* continued to prove a ratings' hit, as men everywhere were encouraged to discover their inner lad. The hallmark of the lad was smoking and drinking too much, a vivid appreciation of the female form and a propensity for curries, lager and not settling down.

Jeremy, although married, was the absolute living embodiment of all this: a grown man whose main interests appeared to be cars, sex and smoking, who was not afraid to take on whoever was in charge. He knew it, too. 'It starts out with a Mild Lad, then Laddism catches on and you get *Loaded* and *Men Behaving Badly*, and you're on the crest of this Lad wave and, in order to stay in front, you're sometimes tempted to go mad and say stupid things,' he confessed. 'But you have to be aware that there are limits. If someone could provide a direct link between something I'd said and someone really getting hurt, things might be different. But until then …' For now, there was to be no change on Planet Jeremy.

He was, however, sometimes bemused by the laddish tag and he was adamant that he had not gone out of his way to cultivate it. 'I don't think I've changed my style, it just happened to coincide with New Laddism, which I was kind of doing before – I was just being me,' he said. 'Then suddenly I had a tag – New Lad. Now there's the temptation to go further than everyone else, but luckily there are producers on *Top Gear* who go, "Er, Jeremy, no." It's amazing how easy people are to upset. When I said that a car snapped knicker elastic at fifty paces, I couldn't believe the furore that was created.' It was, of course, precisely the kind of remark a lad would be expected to make.

And, in 1996, Jeremy scored another coup, by being made a columnist on *The Sun* newspaper. This, of course, gave him a higher profile than ever before, and his laddish humour was perfect for the readers of the paper. Would he buy personalised number plates? 'It's a filthy nouveau thing to do,' said Jeremy, before adding, 'I'd like an amusing one such as DEVIL or PENIS or, best of all, ORGASM.' Did he think cars were as good as sex? 'There's no swelling when I climb into a car, unlike if I was, say, climbing into Claudia Schiffer,' he rather memorably explained. 'And driving a Ferrari isn't as good as bedding Kate

Moss – but it's probably not far off.' Jeremy, incidentally, had a long-term crush on Kate, until she destroyed it some years later.

It was the kind of imagery he frequently used, and to brilliant effect. And when he wasn't comparing cars directly to women, he was judging them on how they would appeal to the opposite sex. 'So the question is,' he once announced, when the Ford Ka appeared on *Top Gear*, 'if you drive this, will people want to have your babies or will they laugh in your face?'

But, contrary to popular opinion, Jeremy's description and analysis of cars did not all revolve around sex. He would use the imagery most consistent with what he was trying to say, and that could be both striking and extremely effective. Indeed, one of the reasons for Clarkson's longstanding popularity with the public is that his imagery when talking about cars was, and is, so often spot on. Take this exchange about the Jaguar and why he likes them: 'People say there's not much space in them, that you're hemmed in, but I think it makes you feel very cosy and safe.' 'Like being in a cockpit?' he was asked. 'No, more like being in a little study with a wood-burning stove. There should be a few books on the walls …'

As Jeremy's profile grew, his wealth also began to accumulate. Despite protestations that he hated the countryside, Jeremy, Francie – who was by now expecting their second child – and Emily, moved out of London to a house in the Cotswolds. Indeed, the family was now acquitting itself with some style: home was a Georgian mansion outside Chipping Norton, which had once belonged to David Sainsbury, a multi-billionaire businessman, peer and Establishment benefactor of art and science trusts. Jeremy might present a laddish image to the world, but that certainly wasn't how he intended to live. Inside, the house was elegantly decorated with a blue-and-white sitting room dominated, rather bizarrely, by a television Jeremy won in a quiz about trivial facts about Yorkshire.

Of course, as befits any successful young couple working in the media, they also had a flat in London. It was in Fulham and Clarkson maintained that he bought it with the specific intention of watching Princess Diana as she made her way in and out of the Harbour Club, which the flat overlooked. 'It's entirely true that I bought the flat so that I could gawp at her,' Clarkson maintained afterwards. 'Ask my wife. Why else would I have chosen a flat overlooking the car park when I could have had one with views over the river? I was a big Diana fan. Then, two weeks after I moved in, she got in a car with a drunken Frenchman and that was the end of that. Terrible.'

And his increasing status was also reflected in his choice of car: having until recently motored around in a much-loved Escort Cosworth – which was given away as the prize in a competition – he had traded up to a Jaguar XJ6 and a Volvo 850R. Indeed, there were no limits to the pursuit of new automotive experiences. For example, he readily admitted to having done up to 186mph in a Lamborghini Countach. His verdict? 'It was absolutely terrifying' – and with that he vowed to do no more than 150mph in the future. His critics, of which there was a growing number, were unimpressed.

But why should he care? Nothing succeeds like success, and Jeremy's life was, pardon the pun, moving up yet another gear.

Shortly after the move, Francie gave birth to the couple's second child, a son, called Finlo. The name, like Finlo's mother, came from the Isle of Man. Francie was then plunged back into the thick of it as she continued to combine the role of wife, mother and Jeremy's manager. When Finlo was only a few months old, Clarkson caused national rage by describing Birmingham as 'a rugby team's bath after they have let the water out', or to put it another way, a circle of scum with nothing at the centre.

This was, of course, vintage Clarkson, but the minor problem this time was that it was said a couple of weeks before the 1996 Motor Show, which was to be held in Birmingham. It didn't seem to worry Jeremy, who came out fighting in favour of the motor industry. 'I love the glitz and glamour of it,' he said. 'You must remember that, after arms and legitimate drugs, the motor industry is the third biggest in the world and when it fluffs up its feathers and puts on a show, it can look pretty good.'

But for all his protestations that his constituency were car buyers rather than car sellers, Clarkson was now considered such an expert on all things motoring that he tended to get dragged into all the major issues of the day. Take the changing face of car manufacturers: once the realm of sexist dinosaurs, their image was evolving into something more acceptable for both sexes – and not before time. Asked if the days when voluptuous women would be seen lying languorously across a car were long gone, Jeremy was adamant that the recent depression in the industry had not just been because of that.

'The trade's been very depressed for the past few years because of all this nonsense about pollution and the need for electric cars,' he said. 'And the motor industry, instead of flexing its enormous muscles and fighting back, has kowtowed and made these tedious little cars. But they've pretty well gone away and it's all back to power and fun and games, and pouting girls.'

On the subject of women, strangely enough, although he has so often compared driving a really good car to having sex, Clarkson is not quite the male chauvinist some perceive him to be. For a start, he has gone on record admitting to nappy changing, which is slightly at odds with the macho image but, more to the point, he has always point blank denied making derogatory remarks about women's driving skills. Indeed, he has quite frequently gone on the record as saying that it's his wife Francie who is the boy racer in the family, not him.

'I've never been sexist, never made remarks about women drivers,' he once said. 'I don't think there is a difference.' It is one area where it would have been so easy to whip up a furore, but Jeremy avoids it. It's only his public image that makes the public think he'd be prejudiced against female motorists – which, at the very least, implies he's a rather more complex character than is sometimes made out.

Another reason for his growing popularity was that, as he continued to explain, he knew no more about the internal workings of cars than the ordinary man on the street. He certainly had a feel for the different models, how they drove, how they reacted and how they actually felt, but as to what actually powered them, he was mystified. He had always been extremely open about this, but now, given that he was probably the most recognisable 'car person' in the country, some people began to wonder if his ignorance was an affectation. Jeremy was keen to reassure them that it wasn't.

'Yeah, people are always keen to talk about that stuff, especially the Germans,' he said. 'They love the details. They love to get you down and say, "Look at our new track rod end. Have you ever seen anything like it?" And I say, "I'm sorry, I don't think it's very important." I don't think the vast majority of people who buy cars care a gnat's what is under the bonnet. Just so long as when they pull out to overtake a tractor, they'll go faster than the tractor.'

So he really didn't understand how engines work? 'I really don't,' Clarkson replied. 'I've tried over the years to understand the basics of internal combustion – how the spark plug has a spark and ignites the fuel mixture, and there's this piston that somehow turns this rod, which turns the gear lever, which makes the car move …' The point was clear. Caustic and witty he might be, but Clarkson was also Everyman.

And his success on television was greater than ever. The public just could not get enough of him, a fact that did not go unnoticed by his bosses at the BBC. Next on the box was to be a series entitled *Jeremy Clarkson Unlimited*, in which the great man got to travel on or in just about everything that moved, not just cars. It was met with the usual Clarkson enthusiasm. 'The basic premise is, if it rolls, floats, flies, shoots a big bullet, runs on high explosive or gasoline, then we feature it,' he explained. But even Jeremy was not superman: he was not actually going to be able to power everything himself. 'I can't fly – though I did go on a powerboat once,' he said. 'The most extraordinary experience. I find it hard to talk about it. I mean it can go from 0–100mph in three seconds. You can't see how half an inch of plywood hull in the water can provoke enough grip to make your face get all twisted up.'

As for the programme itself, though, he was beyond excited. 'It's kind of "Beyond the Dodge Viper" – that was as exciting as cars get, but not as exciting as motorised transport gets,' he said. 'We'll be doing helicopters, gun-ships, powerboats … it should be called "Big Boys' Toys".' It is hard to imagine a more fitting title for all Clarkson's many and varied outings on the television screen.

CHAPTER 5

KING OF
THE ROAD

A long with all the jollity, Jeremy continued to accumulate the various prejudices and hates that remain with him to this day. BMWs – and their drivers – were, and are, a target, and are best summed up in this mid-1990s' tirade 'All BMWs are driven by people who are psychologically unfit to drive anything more powerful than an electric razor. Try it one day, if there is a busy road near to where you live: come to the side turning and see if you can get a BMW to let you out. You'll be let out by a builder's truck; you'll be let out by a bus before you're let out by someone driving a BMW. They're stuck in 1986, urgently dashing to their next meeting. The new 5-series is almost faultless, until you get to the psychopath behind the wheel.' It should be mentioned, in passing, that Francie drove a BMW. It was hard to know which Clarkson was teasing which.

The market for all things Clarkson was booming and so, in

1996, he released an *Unleashed* video, which more than lived up to the name. Jeremy was filmed driving a Volvo into a tree and using a medieval catapult to fling a Nissan Sunny into the ground. The viewers adored it. His detractors, of course, did not.

Another curiosity about Jeremy is that, when you take on the sheer size and numbers of people, car drivers, cars and nationalities he's insulted and then consider the size of his fan base, there must be some crossover. Jeremy has simply been too rude about too many people for there not to have been some category that almost anyone and everyone would fall into, and yet it did nothing at all to hold him back. Quite the opposite in fact: the ruder he got, the more his audience (especially the male part of it) loved him. And they also loved his laddish side, which was absolutely at its height in the mid-1990s.

It was an image Jeremy enjoyed playing up to. Cars, in the Clarkson world view – or at least the ones he promoted on television – were not so much a mode of transport, more a way of getting female attention. 'When you go out, you want to appeal to the opposite sex, and the car is the final touch,' he said on one occasion. 'You see these amazingly stunning people – chiselled jaw, pouting lips and so on – and crap cars. And you think: "You idiot, you're lost, because the car is the only thing we can judge you by. You've gone to all that trouble with the scarf and stubble ensemble, and you're driving a Datsun." You pick up birds in a Ferrari – you just do.'

Speaking of Ferraris … Jeremy had by now acquired one for himself – a red one, naturally – that was his pride and joy. For all the showmanship, the playing to the crowd, the deliberate provocations, there was something almost childlike in Clarkson's appreciation of his new car. A Ferrari is one of the ultimate boy's toys, but it is only the very successful boys that get to own one, and it was the final badge of honour he had been working for. Jeremy had arrived. He had the greatest status symbol on the road: a car sought by millions and owned by the very few. It was the culmination of a dream and Clarkson adored it. He was also rather irritated by the reaction his beautiful new motor so often provoked and it brought on a rare display of grumpiness.

'For most people, it's flash, flash, flash, thumbs up, great car,' he growled. 'But here, it is a peculiarly British thing, some of them think, "Dickhead, wanker, I'll have 'im out of there." Thanks very much, I've only worked seven days a week for ten years with nothing but owning a Ferrari as my goal, and now you're calling me a dickhead. Well, thanks a lot, mate. That sounds awfully Thatcherite, but nothing pisses me off more than envy culture. In America, they see a limo go by and they think, "One day I'll be in one of those." In England they think, "I'll have 'im out of there."'

It was a rare note of aggravation: Jeremy was more than capable of simply laughing off criticism and jealousy from others without a qualm. But when it came to his Ferrari, his pride and joy, it was another matter. It revealed a different side to Clarkson: underneath all the banter and the bonhomie lay someone who could be hurt by criticism, someone who did mind what other people thought about him. And, very tellingly, this aspect to his personality could only be brought out by a very beautiful, and very expensive, car.

And he certainly did love his Ferrari. He was like a child with a toy when he gloated over it. 'It is my favouritest car in the whole wide world,' he crooned. 'Driving it is astonishing. It's like an extension of your hands and feet, really – the tiniest input and it whizzes round like a little rabbit. It's a wonderful car.'

No superlative was good enough for his new motor. 'I went to Italy to drive this new type of Ferrari about three years ago and it was a revelation,' he said on another occasion. 'It was like discovering God. From then on, I just had to have one. I'm afraid I had to put my wife on the streets of King's Cross, get the children up chimneys, sell everything. I just had to have one. It was getting to the point where I used to see cars just as tanks of petrol surrounded by metal. The Ferrari 355 came along and rekindled my interest. It's just so damn good – it's red, of course.'

But his moment of aggravation was not the end of it. Jeremy even let on that he sometimes worried that being a car aficionado could be, well, a bit anoraky, but that he was greatly relieved to see that it wasn't when he looked at the other people who appreciated their vehicles. 'Steve Coogan, Robbie Coltrane, Alexei Sayle – as soon as they've got a bit of money, they sneak off and buy a car,' he said. 'Makes you feel better, makes you feel like you're not a complete animal when you find that quite trendy people are into cars as well.' So was Clarkson experiencing self-doubt? It's not a moment that has been repeated that often since.

One constant in Jeremy's life, of course, was Francie. Completely different in her views to those of her husband, she continued to keep him grounded, something he is only too keen to acknowledge. And the fact that she is so level-headed provides a contrast to the public side of his life, which became increasingly frenetic as his fame grew. 'Put it this way, she comes in every night with a copy of the *Big Issue*,' he said. 'She used to counsel people who'd just been made redundant. I would give her tips for the day, such as telling them to pull themselves together and stop whinging. You could say she's mellowed me.'

That slightly softer Jeremy also came through when talking about another of his cars – this one, a Volvo. Was Jeremy himself a superlative driver? At this he came across as downright modest. 'I'm a perfectly ordinary driver with a clean licence who doesn't speed except when on a racetrack when there's a camera pointed at me,' he said. 'For the rest of the time, I just potter. I have an automatic, bright red Volvo with a baby seat that looks staid but can do 160mph. [But] when a car goes into a spin, I tend to undo the safety belt and climb in the back.' It was this streak of self-deprecation that stopped him from coming across as just too arrogant, and it is something Clarkson has perfected over the years. Say something shocking about whatever subject you like, and then say something that shows you really don't take yourself too seriously. It is a formula Jeremy has got down to a fine art.

As his popularity grew and grew, offers were flooding in and, increasingly, they had little or nothing to do with cars. Clarkson was by now a fully fledged TV personality: he was no longer famous for just being a motoring expert, but for his abrasive personality and forthright views. And those qualities made him suitable for a wide range of programmes, not just *Top Gear* and

...e numerous one-off series he now presented that were also to do with cars.

But not all offers were suitable. When you reach the level of celebrity he has attained, producers are desperate to haul you into anything, as your name alone becomes a draw. Sometimes, however, it is hard to escape the impression that these producers have not really thought the offers through. Jeremy was particularly taken aback when asked to front one show – *Gladiators*, which at the time was one of the most successful shows on TV. 'I'm too fat,' said a slightly incredulous Clarkson. 'They'd call me the Lardiator. I thought it was a joke when I got the offer; it took me three days to come around.

'Can you imagine me on *Gladiators*? I'd be absolutely hopeless. The Gladiators are super fit – I'm as fat as a hippopotamus. I'd be exhausted just walking from one end of the arena to another. I'm the least fit person in the world. I've never worked out and have no wish to start. I was very flattered to have been asked. I would have enjoyed working with Ulrika. It would have been a laugh – well, for me, anyway.'

By October 1997, interest in Jeremy was now at such a fever pitch that his wife was getting dragged into the limelight, too. And not only that: she was venturing into Jeremy's territory. As his manager, Francie was bound to have had some knowledge about cars, if only through osmosis, but in actual fact she was as keen on cars as her husband. He often joked that it was she who liked going to motor shows and she who was the fast driver in the house, which was fortunate, given the extent to which the Clarkson household revolved around cars.

Francie is also an extremely spirited woman, as witnessed by the fact that now she was taking to the road herself, by participating in the Liège-Agadir-Liège International Touring Trial, organised by the Guild of Motor Endurance. It was her first rally and her partner was to be Emma Stanford. The two were driving a Technic Speedster, a car that very much resembled a Porsche, despite the fact that Francie, like her husband, cheerfully proclaimed she knew nothing about the internal workings of cars. This was, in fact, to be the first of many rallies in which she took part. It was, perhaps, a way of maintaining her independence: once a year she got away from the family and took to the road on her own.

As Clarkson's fame grew, so too did his wealth. Despite his professed loathing of the countryside, the Cotswold house was clearly a good base for the family, as it provided room both for the growing brood of children and the growing collection of cars. There was also plenty of room for Jeremy and Francie to enjoy themselves: a stable complex provided both garage space and a games room, complete not only with a dartboard and ping-pong table, but with two Sega rally machines – that is, virtual cars on virtual backgrounds, which you sit in a machine and play. They, too, were boys' toys par excellence and gave the whole family hours of pleasure in the evenings.

'Francie bought them for my birthday,' Clarkson explained, as he demonstrated how the machines work. 'Basically, you can just race each other round and round. We just get very, very drunk at night and then race cars. Look! There's a choice of a Lancia or a Toyota. You can go absolutely flat out, very,

...y drunk all night long. It is good fun, getting it out of your system. I've got a rear view mirror and I can see the other one coming up behind me. I'll have a crash! Look! I'm going at 260 kilometres an hour!' This particular toy seemed to be almost as much fun as the Ferrari.

At around this time, there was a rather surprising and touching rapprochement between Jeremy and his old school. Repton, it seems, had been concerned that Jeremy hated the old place, and various masters had been assuring people that Clarkson had not actually been expelled, presumably as a way of making him feel better about the past. As a tactic, that particular one didn't work. According to the man himself, oh yes he had been thrown out. Indeed, it was a matter of pride.

'I saw an article in which my old school was quoted as saying I hadn't been expelled,' he said. 'Well I was – for a whole chapter of lawbreaking. I just didn't do anything they wanted me to do. I have a letter confirming that I was thrown out and that I would never be welcome on the school premises again as long as I lived.' But despite both the expulsion and the school's subsequent denial of it, he was more than willing to build bridges again. 'I'd love to go back,' he said. 'But I don't want to offer. That sounds awfully pretentious. They obviously think that because I keep telling people I got expelled I've got something against Repton. But I haven't – they were the five happiest years of my life; I loved them.'

His past was to come up again in a different form, this time a very unexpected one. Jeremy and his *Top Gear* colleague Steve Berry had been trading the odd on-screen insult, but now, for reasons that were not entirely clear, the friction boiled over into real life. Steve launched an astonishing attack on Clarkson and was particularly withering about his reputation as a rebel at school.

'I wake up each morning and hope Jeremy will disappear down a big hole in the ground,' he said. 'There's nothing about him that I like. He dresses appallingly, likes long-haired seventies rock bands and he's got the worst hairstyle in Britain since Kevin Keegan stopped having that terrible perm. He's created this image out of nothing, but really he's just a middle-class boy who's a bit sad. He thinks he's a rebel because he sneaked away to town for a couple of pints of cider and got expelled from an expensive public school. Where I come from, bad behaviour is joy riding and dealing heroin, cocaine and Ecstasy.

'He's managed to create a cottage industry from his image and has made a lot of money, but basically it's all a sham. His antics at school amount to nothing more than Bunteresque schoolboy japes ... making apple-pie beds for the headmaster, refusing to fag for the sixth formers and smoking cigarettes behind the dorm. And, as for his boasts with girls, I bet if one had come on to Jeremy when he was at school, he'd have run a mile.'

With that, Steve turned to analysing the difference between Jeremy and himself. 'Clarkson receives a load of hate mail, but I get letters from women who want me to father their children,' he explained. 'A lot of Jeremy's mail has to be vetted by the BBC because so many of the viewers take exception to him. But I get letters that say, "Dear Steve, I'm a happily married woman with three children, but I dream of the day you'll arrive outside my three-bed semi on a hugely powerful motorcycle, clad from head to toe in black leather, and whisk me away for a life of sex, drugs and rock and roll!"

'We give each other' – by this time Steve was talking about Jeremy again, not the happily married housewife – 'a load of stick when we're working together. He was taking the mick out of me on TV the other day, so I returned the compliment. I said on-air, "The heaviest part of any car is the engine – unless, of course, Jeremy is driving it, because he is a bit of a porker."'

It is difficult to know what provoked this. It's possible, of course, that Steve was only joking, but it didn't really come across as such. It's also possible that he thought this would create some extra publicity for the show. As for Clarkson himself, he was mystified. 'I'm shocked by this,' he said. 'There has never been anything to provoke this sort of outburst. I can't think what I've done to offend Steve in this way. I never realised he didn't like me.'

This attack, however, certainly didn't put Clarkson off his stride. Indeed, he seemed keener than ever to take on daredevil missions on television, with his next venture entitled *Extreme Machines*, a series of trials of some of the fastest vehicles in the world. This really was serious boys' toys territory: Jeremy and his crew were to try out everything from snowmobiles and hydroplanes to Formula One powerboats, New Zealand Zorb balls and Second World War P-51 Mustangs. This was not for the faint-hearted and along the way the crew had some very nasty incidents. The cameraman's plane ran out of fuel in mid-flight, the soundman had a heart attack while scaling a 40ft supertanker and everyone was caught in an alligator-infested swamp in Florida.

Jeremy was quite open about the fact that it was not an easy ride. The worst bit, he said, came when he went in a US Air Force F-15. 'I had no idea just how violent the effects of the G-forces were going to be,' he said. 'I was violently sick inside the cockpit after one high-speed manoeuvre and when I got out after the 90-minute ride I just collapsed. I couldn't talk, think or sit up and it took me all day to recover. It's the first time in my life I've been lost for words.'

He certainly did seem to have been slightly shaken by the experience. 'You wear these trousers that explode,' he said. 'When the G-force starts, compressed air shoots into them to tighten everything up and stop the blood from going into your legs. It is quite disconcerting: they just go bang! [But] when you are in the heavens, you don't have the sensation of speed that you have when you are in a car, or when you are close to the ground. He [the pilot] did at one stage take me very low and then accelerated very fast. He climbed from 1,000ft to 18,000ft in eleven seconds. You can't even conceive of what that does to your ears.'

That was not the only ordeal in the making of the series. On another occasion, Jeremy and his crew were on a swamp buggy in Florida when disaster struck. 'One minute we were whizzing along and the next we had capsized in alligator-infested waters,' said Clarkson. 'You've never seen four people scrambling to get out of the water so quickly. Luckily, we got out before the alligators got to us, but we never saw the cameras and other equipment again.'

And in case viewers were left in any doubt as to how wearing all of this really was, his colleague Murray Clarke actually had a heart attack while filming the series. 'It was dreadful because we all had to get off this tanker via a rope ladder in the middle of the sea,' Jeremy recalled. 'Murray's a very fit guy, but he had a heart attack that put him in hospital for three months.' All told, the entire team was glad when the filming was over. 'I'm just glad to be back without anyone getting killed,' Jeremy said.

The experience did leave a mark. No one could have accused Clarkson of boasting about his physical courage, for he was adamant that he didn't have any. 'It was really scary, but something I'm glad I did, because when I'm sitting on a porch in my eighties with a single malt, I'll be able to tell my grandchildren,' he said. 'The trouble with making these programmes is I have pipe cleaners for arms, a beer gut and smoke too much. I'm Mr Timid, who even holds on to the banister when walking downstairs.'

Again, however, another side of Jeremy briefly came to light. He was now bona fide both rich and famous, but it seemed to bring on at least moments of introspection. He had come in for a great deal of teasing about his sometimes lascivious remarks about cars, and seemed to be giving some thought as to what the sexual connotation of a car really is.

'Man's relationship with a car is an interesting one,' he said, when asked about the subject. 'I don't know where the sexual side of it comes in – all this stuff about E-types with bonnets like penises – I've never really understood that.' But had not Clarkson revelled in exactly that type of description? Not according to him. 'Cheap sexual metaphors,' he said of his style of presenting. 'Muriel Gray said the other day, "All you do for a living is make cheap sexual metaphors." So I've stopped. And it was becoming easy – it is jolly easy to say, "This car snaps knicker elastic at twenty paces", or "If this car were a women it would be Daryl Hannah." But I've done it now. I've got to think of new ways of describing cars – I'm in limbo at the moment. I'm probably being a bit dull.'

It was an interesting conundrum: how to get the very sense of the car across while staying verbally on the straight and narrow. Jeremy was in brooding mode. 'The excitement of the car is the speed of it,' he said. 'That's the essence of it, isn't it? But you can't just say, "This car is fast," or, "This car does 186 miles an hour." You have to explain what it feels like to be in a deckchair on a quiet, peaceful afternoon and a Boeing 747 flies into the small of your back. That is what acceleration feels like. You have to find new ways to describe it.'

But he couldn't resist a return to the imagery for which he had become so well known. 'Treat your car like a metal overcoat and think about what style you want to project,' he argued. 'There's no need anymore for any long, phallic bonnets. If you drive one of those big people carriers with eight seats, it's like, "Hey, mine works fine, mate. Look at all my children."'

And the Clarkson collection of cars was itself building up. To the amusement of some onlookers, Francie's BMW had come to the attention of the public; Jeremy grumbled slightly, but was fairly restrained. Indeed, he bordered on the complimentary. 'It is an amazing car,' he said. 'The doors don't open, they drop down. You push this button and the whole thing goes bzzzz and shoots down there so you can drive along with the doors down. It's not my idea of perfection, of course,' he said, suddenly remembering himself, 'because it is a BMW. I'm not very fond of BMWs – they tend to be driven by plonkers.'

Jeremy's family life was, in fact, a settled and happy part of his life. The Clarksons had discovered that it worked so well to have Francie act as her husband's manager that, far from keeping them under one another's feet, it produced a good working relationship as well as a successful private one. 'It works beautifully,' said Francie. 'I have an office at home and manage all Jeremy's affairs. My admin skills weren't up to much in the beginning, but I've got quite proficient and I've always been good with money.'

If truth be told, it was actually, contrary to appearances, Jeremy who was the stickler for routine, while Francie was more chaotic. 'He's like the reverse of what they say about swans,' said Francie. 'Jeremy glides along below the surface, but he's paddling like mad above it. He may give the impression of seeming rather shambolic in his approach to life, but in reality he's little short of a perfectionist. He is completely organised and a stickler for meeting every deadline. The truth is, I'm the chaotic one and I'm supposed to be the one that runs him.'

This impression was reinforced by another Clarkson outburst, this one about timekeeping. Indeed, it made him sound more like a crusty old habitué of a traditional gentleman's club than TV's bad boy. 'It's so rude,' he said on the subject of lateness. Nor did he take it kindly when people thought he really was a monster. 'People think I bite the heads off chickens, that I can never be anywhere on time, that I don't care a fig about anything, that I'm a poor father. But that's not me. Just ask Francie.'

He was, in fact, becoming increasingly domesticated. In public, the Clarkson image continued to be that of the wild man but at home, it was quite a different story. Jeremy was a devoted father and did his bit with the children, although, as Francie explained, there were limits. Asked if he was a good father, she replied, 'Absolutely brilliant. [But] he announced from the outset that he just couldn't deal with poo. I told him that was fine – I couldn't deal with sick.'

'It isn't just me being silly,' interjected Jeremy. 'Even seeing a dirty nappy makes me physically gag. So I've never changed either of the children's nappies.'

Except once. 'My sister had been ill and I'd got home from seeing her a bit later than I'd said,' explained Francie. 'There was Jeremy, with one of those Yasser Arafat-type scarves drenched in Chanel wrapped round his mouth, a snorkel mask over his eyes and nose and a pair of Marigold gloves on his hands. He'd been undressing Emily for her bath and discovered a full nappy.'

On other occasions, incidentally, Clarkson was a bit more laid-back about the whole area: when asked if he'd ever changed a nappy, he replied, 'It has been known.'

However, all that just put him at one with the men who admired him: like him, they were middle-class fathers, trying to combine work with the demands of being a new man, nappy changing and all. His tastes were fairly Middle England,

hey did lean rather more towards Tom Clancy
Dickens. Indeed, the former ranked as one of his
velists. 'I have two [favourites],' he said. 'Tom Clancy
and Nick Hornby. Nick Hornby is funny – I loved his *High
Fidelity*, and Tom Clancy's books are very, very exciting. Kids
should be reading books like that in schools, not Shakespeare,
when you can't even understand the language.' Shakespeare
was to come in for a bit of aggro, as well, when Clarkson was
championing Isambard Kingdom Brunel as the greatest ever
Briton and Shakespeare was one of the other contenders. But
more of that later.

Meanwhile, the country continued to lap up information
about Clarkson's tastes. His most treasured book? '*Monty Python's
Big Red Book*, which was signed by all of them,' he replied. 'My
dad knew John Cleese years ago – they met in a restaurant in
Earl's Court. I was about fourteen and a colossal Monty Python
fan; I still am. I was taken to see them backstage and went out
to dinner with them.'

His taste in what he watched on the box was much in the
same vein. 'Mostly films, apart from the *Fast Show*, which is
obviously unmissable, as is Steve Coogan's Alan Partridge, which
I rank alongside *Monty Python*, *Fawlty Towers* and *Blackadder*,' he
said. This was practically Middle England, or at least men of a
certain age in Middle England, made flesh. Jeremy was not only
popular with the viewers, but his tastes were exactly like theirs.
Was it any wonder he got mobbed now wherever he went?

It went on. His radio station of choice? 'Largely Virgin
Radio in London,' said Clarkson. 'But I can't get it at home

in Chipping Norton so – this is embarrassing – I've started listening to Radio 2.' And what soap opera would he most like to live in? 'Dallas. I wouldn't want to live in any of the places the British soaps are set in. There should be one in Fulham, with nice properties and agreeable people.' It was all very middle class – and ultra safe at that.

But you can't keep a good lad down. Clarkson occasionally grumbled that people only ever saw the laddish side to him and no one ever realised he was a grown-up man with an estate in the country and two children, but then he did himself sometimes conform to that stereotype. When asked about his favourite music for the car, no one should have been surprised at the answer: 'I have a collection of good seventies' rock bands, Oasis' *(What's The Story) Morning Glory?* and a collection of James Bond hits,' he said. 'Believe it or not, I am rather a slow driver – my wife says I dawdle. So when I'm in a hurry, I put on a James Bond and I get home quicker.'

Nor could you keep his opinions tucked away for long. Asked who he would like to serve him breakfast in bed, Clarkson replied, 'Other than my wife? Tony Blair. I took the train the other day and it was ridiculously late. I'd say, "No more grinning, Tony, just build some roads."' And his first act as world leader? 'I'd get rid of the USA and Switzerland,' he somewhat mysteriously announced. 'They wouldn't be allowed to be countries; I might cover them with sea. After that, I'd get rid of all the bus lanes in the world.'

CHAPTER 6

LIFE IN THE FAST LANE

His image was now set in stone: a devoted motorist who loved fast cars, loved driving, was not overly concerned about the environment and pretty much felt that, environmentally speaking, the planet could look after itself. Or was it? Much to the shock of just about everyone, Jeremy – who once remarked that bicycles should be taxed 'For hogging a third of the road' – was quite suddenly outed as being a cyclist himself. In the process, he became the subject of some good-natured teasing. 'It is a terrible and unexpected shock,' said his friend and fellow *Top Gear* presenter Quentin Willson. 'He has never once mentioned owning a bike to me. Perhaps he's a budding environmentalist – think of our ratings!'

Clarkson took it on the chin. 'I admit to having cycled about five miles a day for the last month, but I don't like it and it has nothing to do with the environment,' he admitted, as it was revealed that his shameful vehicle was a twenty-one-gear Raleigh mountain bike. 'I was recently described as looking like Stephen Fry's older, fatter sister. Now I'm lithe, like a racing snake.'

And, as a further sign of the biter bitten, Clarkson went on to reveal that a gang of youths in a car had yelled taunts at him when he was on his bike. 'One of them leaned out the window and suggested that my seed fell on fallow ground,' he said. 'When they realised who I was, they turned around and shouted the same thing, but inserted the word "turncoat" in front of it.'

Francie — who had let the secret out in the first place — leapt to her husband's defence. 'To be frank, his behaviour is getting worse, not better,' she assured an appalled public. 'He has starting scouring the countryside for beef on the bone and he has a loathing for anything green.'

By now, the story was assuming a momentum of its own. It is hard to think of anyone else in the country who could have got such extensive coverage merely for riding a bicycle (with the possible exception of the then eccentric Mayor of London and former editor of *The Spectator* Boris Johnson), but Jeremy was now so well known as a basher of all things green that this really was deemed newsworthy. Clarkson's friend Andy Willman, who had produced *Extreme Machines*, joined in the fun. He was equally determined that this had nothing to do with looking after nature. 'I accept the bike thing is shocking,' he said. 'He has definitely not been talking about it, but I'd say it had more to do with his gut than the environment at large.'

The local villagers thoroughly enjoyed hearing the news. 'The bike will certainly be very different from his red Ferrari,' said Jeremy Catling of the nearby Cotswolds newsagents. 'People in the town stand gawping at it, but I can't see them doing that with a bike.'

Gwyn Osborn, landlord of the Wagon and Horses in the village, said, 'I think a bike will make a pleasant change for him. He might enjoy it once he gets used to it. For my money, it's good that he is doing his bit for the environment.' Clarkson's views on that last point are unknown.

In actual fact, there are signs that Clarkson's attitude towards the environment is rather more ambiguous than he publicly lets on. He will certainly say and do anything that comes to mind to raise the hackles of the environmental lobby – and given the sometimes sanctimonious nature of their protestations, his actions are not altogether without merit – but Jeremy is not a foolish man. He himself has children and is thus as concerned as anyone about the future of the world. Sometimes he has mentioned the Arctic ice cap melting and, of the cars he drives, not all of them are gas-guzzling road hogs. But he would never, ever let on that green issues hold any interest for him whatsoever: he cultivates the image that he has no intention of allowing it to soften.

The same applies to so much of his public image. He can talk about cars that snap knicker elastic until the cows come home, and yet there is no evidence whatsoever that he is genuinely sexist. As he himself was at pains to point out, his life was run by a woman – his wife. And then there's the fact that the parent he most closely resembles is his mother. But given his image, and he doesn't do a lot to counteract this view of him, people tend to assume he's chauvinistic. In actual fact, he's not.

Soon he was in the papers again, although in this case it was someone else's actions rather than his own that made the headlines. And what a disillusioning time it was for him, too. Jeremy had long been a fan of the model Kate Moss, frequently describing her as one of the most beautiful and desirable women in the world, and so, at the London première of Steve Coogan's *The Man Who Thinks He's It*, he was utterly delighted to see Kate was present, too. Judging his moment, he went up to her, held out a hand and said, 'Hi, I'm Jeremy Clarkson. I do *Top Gear*.'

Kate looked confused. 'Are you trying to sell me drugs?' she asked.

That exchange has gone down in the annals of show-business history as one of the all-time misunderstandings, and it had another consequence too – Clarkson's crush on Kate ended then and there. 'I'd never met Kate Moss before,' he said afterwards. 'To be honest, I didn't really know who anyone was in her party – they were all far too young for me.' He certainly knew who she was, though, and must have thought it the opportunity of a lifetime to finally be able to say hello.

It was an intensely amusing moment for the onlookers. 'It was a very funny exchange,' said one witness to the event. 'Jeremy was keen to say hello to Kate, but was mystified by her response. She just looked very strangely at him and asked him if he was talking about drugs. Everyone around them just fell about laughing. Noel Gallagher was sitting with Kate and was killing himself at her mistake. She saw the funny side, too – once she realised what Jeremy meant.'

It was a slight blow to the ego, however. Not only did Kate not have the faintest idea who Jeremy was, but she had clearly never heard of the programme, either. It would have been better, far, far better, if they had never met.

Clarkson himself, meanwhile, was up to his old tricks again, causing upset and outrage everywhere he went. First, he announced that everyone who rode a scooter was clearly homosexual. The next furore came at that October's Motor Show in Birmingham, when Jeremy took part in a quiz on the *Top Gear* stand. He kicked off by commenting, 'The British motor industry is really owned by Nazis', before nearly causing an international incident by upsetting the Koreans on a nearby stand. Jeremy accused the Hyundai staff of eating dogs and, for good measure, added that the Hyundai XG model itself was a 'dog's dinner'.

This did not go down well and the ensuing row was on a scale that was large even for Jeremy. 'Clarkson said the people on our stand had eaten dog – as the company is Korean – and that the designer of one of our cars, the XG, had eaten a spaniel,' said Stephen Kitson, head of Hyundai's public relations. 'Our staff on the stand, which is right next to *Top Gear*'s, have been offended. We feel the comments are bigoted and racist and vindictive.' Clarkson had almost certainly not meant his comments to be taken so seriously – he frequently gives the appearance of amazement that anyone ever listens to a word he has to say, but again, he clearly couldn't help himself. A politically incorrect joke popped into his mind and he made it.

But it wasn't taken that lightly by everyone else. Indeed, Hyundai were so offended that they complained to the then-BBC director general John Birt, while the organisers of the Motor Show had words with the *Top Gear* team. This did not worry Jeremy, who the next day advised visitors to the show who had their dogs with them to avoid the Hyundai stand. 'They'll sprinkle some ketchup on the poor thing's back, and the next thing you know you'll have an empty lead,' he said. Cue absolute outrage. There have been frosty moments between Clarkson and Hyundai ever since. Jeremy, needless to say, has been unrepentant.

As in the above exchange, though, it is hard not to feel that the joke is on those who get hot under the collar. For a start, Clarkson was not being serious. Secondly, he was trying – successfully – to rile the people that he did. Thirdly, in this and many other controversies, it is Jeremy's opponent who comes across as being utterly po-faced, both for lacking a sense of humour and for taking themselves too seriously. Better by far to let him make his jokes and have done with it.

It was easy to see why Clarkson sometimes became so irritated by the people who got worked up about what he had to say. Of the frequent charges of sexism, he was quite blunt with one interviewer. 'This is just pathetic,' he said. 'Your life must be so shallow if you can watch the news and see that the Americans have blown up a baby food factory, discover the Arctic's melting, and you then get whipped up about me saying,

"This'll snap your knicker elastic." It's extraordina
to concede he had a point – as well as making referei.
concerns about global warming.

There were, by now, almost two Clarksons. First, there w
the aggressive, rude, motormouthed Jeremy, but these days there
was also the country-dwelling squire of the manor, with six
acres of countryside and a growing collection of cars. There was
the Ferrari – who could forget the Ferrari? Jeremy certainly
couldn't. 'It's kinetic art and I'd put it in the sitting room if the
sitting room was large enough,' he once said. 'I've made a lot of
sacrifices to buy it and, at the moment, I could sell it for more
than it cost, but I expect the market will collapse and I'd be left
looking a ninny. I don't subscribe to pensions and I'd rather
enjoy a Ferrari than a piece of paper telling me how much my
investments are worth. You have only 600,000 hours to live and
I don't want to be bored for a minute.'

That was clearly his life philosophy. But these days, there were
other cars too. Jeremy was also the proud driver of a Jaguar XJR:
'The nicest thing is that you can pull up outside an expensive
West End hotel and the doorman will scuttle out and open the
door, and yet, in south London, it won't be touched because
people assume you're a drug dealer. I think I'm a bit too young
for it.' It was also on permanent loan to Jeremy, as opposed to a
car he had bought himself, something he admitted very nearly
amounted to a freebie. 'It's a borderline case, I must confess,' he
said. 'I come from Yorkshire, where, if someone asks, "Do you
want a free car?" the answer is, "Yes, on the understanding that
if it falls to bits I'll write about that."'

But Jeremy was adamant that, on the whole, he avoided such things. The motor industry was only too keen to butter up as many journalists as it could by organising fantastic journeys, opportunities and promotional events, which Clarkson thought better left untouched. 'Bundles of cash aren't pushed across the table, but there's a lot of corporate hospitality, which I avoid like a rabid dog,' he said. 'It's, "Come to the south of France, first class; stay in the Carlton; drive the car for an hour and we'll tip champagne and caviar down your throat for days on end." I wish they'd just send the car round. I haven't time to listen to PRs spouting rubbish for hours. The minute they open their mouths, you put your fingers in your ears and hum. It's far better to keep at arm's length from the car world.'

It was this kind of attitude that gave him the authority to speak as he did. For all the entertainment factor in Clarkson's work, it is often forgotten that he would never have got where he is today had he not actually been a very good reporter in the industry. Clarkson is loved and loathed in equal measures, but no one doubts his integrity. In fact, it's a measure of the man that he is completely trusted when it comes to cars: for all the protestations that no one listens to what he says, the fact is that they do. They are aware that he will not have had his head turned by the lavish hospitality that is part of that world: he will speak his mind and give his opinion as befits the blunt northerner that he still is.

It was the summer of 1998 and a new programme was in the offing, this one called *Waterworld*. As the title suggests, this time it was about the machines that travel on water. 'It remains to be seen how much viewers can take of a speed boat or yacht whizzing along, but it's been great fun because I've always loved boats more than cars,' Clarkson said. 'The sea is designed for fish, not boats, so you're not only taking on a machine, but trying to tame the elements. It's a free-for-all. There are no speed limits. You can drink and drive – some are paralytic, which isn't a good idea – but it's nice to be allowed to make up your own mind rather than having Mr Blair and Mr Prescott interfering.'

The image of Clarkson as a man of the seas is a convincing one. But the multiple challenges he was setting himself were what he was really enjoying. Yes, he was now seeing how well he could handle a boat. But he was also setting himself a new task, as he did whenever he tried out a new venture: to take the viewer with him. More and more the success or otherwise of these programmes hung on Clarkson himself, for they were as much vehicles for him as they were programmes about their subject matter. And, in the competitive world of television, anything that didn't work well would have been pounced on and his reputation damaged.

By this time, however, there really was no one else working in the industry who could touch him. None of the other motoring correspondents had anything like the draw he did, and none had been able to cross over so successfully into more mainstream TV. Nor were there many presenters who could pull in the viewers merely on account of their names. But Jeremy was now one of them: with him on board, a programme was guaranteed at least a viewing and, in a great many cases, success.

With this increasing success, however, Jeremy had lost none

of his power to irritate and cause trouble. Media mogul Janet Street-Porter was the latest to chip in: 'If I really want to make myself ill, I think about Jeremy Clarkson,' she announced. Clarkson responded by saying he hoped wolves would be reintroduced into the countryside and that one would eat her. The public lapped it up. Jeremy was clearly unafraid to take on anyone – and was also extremely creative when he returned fire.

Nonetheless, it did sometimes worry people that he would misbehave in the wrong circumstances. For all the complaints about the state of television today, in some quarters it is still remarkably staid and there were people who were seriously concerned that one day Clarkson would go too far. On the one hand, he was sought after as a television presence, particularly when fronting a programme but, on the other, there was nervousness about letting him live on air. Would he do or say something totally unacceptable? Almost certainly not, for Clarkson was nothing if not professional, but that was not enough to assuage some fears.

Even Judy Finnegan was cautious and said she didn't want him on *Good Morning*. Clarkson was bemused. 'She was obviously worried I'd swear and break wind,' he said. Understandably, he drew attention to the fact that he was now a married father, not a young yob bigging it up of a Saturday night. 'I'm called a lad, but I'm thirty-eight and my hair's falling out,' he went on. 'On *Top Gear*, we're middle-aged men with families, who arrive at the office saying, "It was great last night. Went home, had supper in front of the telly, and was in bed by eleven." Very laddish!'

Above all, though, the day job continued to thrill. Jeremy

adored cars more than ever, an enthusiasm he effortlessly communicated to the audience. For years now he had been presenting *Top Gear*, and yet he still came across as fresh, as passionate and as knowledgeable about the subject as ever. And much as he might object to still being seen as a lad in some quarters, he had no problem whatsoever when it came to associating him with cars. He remained transfixed by the image that a particular car conveyed, as well as how well it actually moved, and continued to bang this message across.

'I don't mind being typecast with cars – it's more fun than flowers or duvets – and I'm still thrilled whenever I get into a new one, even if it's cheap and from Poland,' he said. 'The real challenge is, "How can I convey this car?" They're mostly fast, reliable and economical, so you have to ask, "What does it say about you?" Some drivers spend a fortune on personal appearance and then buy a crappy car. You think, "No, no, no." In a traffic jam it is a full metal yashmak, the only clue as to what sort of person you are.'

Despite the caution of some television executives, Clarkson's popularity was now in the stratosphere. If anything, his growing rudeness endeared him even more to his particular fan base. This popularity was now such that it allowed him to branch out into other fields, too, as demand for him grew across the industry. Details were initially unclear, but it emerged that a new type of television show was on the cards, one that had nothing to do with cars or, indeed, any other kind of moving vehicle.

He had risen above the programme that launched him: it was

no longer just Jeremy Clarkson of *Top Gear*, but Jeremy Clarkson as a character and personality in his own right. He was proving that he could stay the course too. Unlike many celebrities, he had not buckled under the pressure, let it go to his head or made one of the myriad mistakes that can cause problems. He had also proved himself more than capable of taking the flack he so frequently encountered, knowing that if he upset people they were bound to shout back and all he needed to do was to open his mouth to cause a furore from some sector of the population. Controversy followed him everywhere – and he liked it that way.

So it was no surprise that when details first began to emerge about his next project, it was clear that this was going to be a different type of show. Despite the undoubted strengths he brought with him to his work, up until now – as he frequently said himself – the programmes he presented could have been done by another man. *Top Gear*, *Extreme Machines* and the rest were certainly perfect shows for him to work on, but they didn't exist purely because Jeremy was there to front them: they were concepts in their own right. Now, however, it looked as if a new kind of project was on the horizon, one specifically tailored to cater to the strengths of its front man. Initially, despite the added pressure this would bring, Clarkson was very calm.

'I'm very busy and sometimes think I've overdone it,' he said. 'I never had any aspirations. Ambition seems to be a worry. You either achieve it, in which case, so what? Or you don't and you're disappointed. There's nothing I ever really want to do, which means I'm never going to be disappointed. If it all goes wrong tomorrow, and it will – my teeth will turn yellow with nicotine, my hair will fall out and I won't be able to think of anything interesting to say – I'll put the past few years in a box, label it, "A good time" and shove it in the loft. I'm quite practical about everything.'

But this casual attitude didn't last. Towards the end of 1998, it was announced that he was going to get his very own chat show on BBC Two called, as logic would dictate, *Clarkson*. Jeremy affected great concern at the opprobrium that would almost certainly be heaped on him from the moment the show first aired, and then couldn't resist bringing up both the gay scooter and the Hyundai incidents again, as examples of why people might hate him.

It was an interesting idea. There have only ever been two real maestros of the British chat show – Terry Wogan and Michael Parkinson – and so to bring a very different kind of interviewer to the screen was something of a gamble on the BBC's part. But it was not as outlandish as it looked. Like Parkinson, Clarkson had actually started as a journalist, and understood how to go about getting information out of the people he would be meeting on screen. The BBC was also clearly hoping that Clarkson's controversial streak would strike some interesting debate – something singularly lacking in the British chat show to date – as well as sparky television. And he certainly had a personality that could command the small screen.

But a chat show is not an easy vehicle in which to shine, as television presenters too numerous to mention had discovered before now. It requires a mix of strong personality yet an ability to stand back from the centre stage, something that is extremely difficult to pull off. Jeremy might have the ability to start a row with one of his guests, but would he be able to get them to tell him anecdotes, and would his sheer presence be overwhelming? Clarkson is, after all, a very big man, and that, as much as his ability to have an argument, can actually make some people very nervous of him.

But whatever doubts anyone else might have were more than matched by the man himself. Clarkson was as self-deprecating as ever, and really did appear to be having an attack of nerves. This was completely different from anything he'd done before and it was more pressurised, too. Unlike all the others he had done, this programme would stand or fall because of its presenter, not his subject matter, which meant that attention was going to be focused on Clarkson as never before.

His many detractors would be itching for it to fail, while at the same time it would say a great deal about Jeremy's future in the industry. Could he be a stalwart of the business, able to take on any number of different types of programming, or would he be lost without his props – the cars and other machines – and not be able to go it alone? The more he was able to branch out into different strands of television, the better it would be for his career in the long term. But equally, a high-profile flop could do him some serious damage. Clarkson understood just what was at stake.

'There is a world of difference between doing a poky motoring programme on BBC Two and being a presenter,' he said. 'The chat show may be the only thing that sorts it out, which is another reason why I am so worried. If [people] are watching *Top Gear*, it is because they're interested in cars. But suddenly I'm in a studio doing an opening monologue and it's just me. I've suddenly got to become a lot more interesting in the next few months.' That last comment, however, was a little disingenuous. Clarkson was chosen to do the show precisely because he had such a forceful personality.

Nervous he might have been, but he was becoming seriously wealthy with it. Estimates now put his annual salary at about £500,000, and the Clarksons continued to live in some style. In some ways that made what he was about to do riskier still: he had built a fortune on one type of programme and he was not going to try something completely different without careful consideration. Jeremy was hugely popular among a large section of the population, but if this went badly – and, of course, there was a chance that it would – then he risked ruining his reputation and with it losing his fan base. But Clarkson was not a man to avoid a challenge.

'When you're filming things like cars, if you run out of things to say, you just whizz round with some music going and shut up,' he said. 'So suddenly, the idea of sitting there, just me, without my new Lamborghini or any of my other props – it's scary. People who watch *Top Gear* aren't tuning in to see me; they're tuning in to see the cars. If I did a programme on newt farming, no one would watch.'

Indeed, so adamant was Clarkson about his qualms that right up until the very last minute he maintained he was going to turn the new programme down. 'I drove down to London to the final push meeting they'd arranged to see if I'd change my mind, and all the way down I was saying to myself, "No, no, no, no! I am not doing a chat show. There are a million people who can do that. There's Jonathan Ross, Chris Evans and Michael Parkinson – they do those. I go in Jags and things; that's my job. No, no, no!" I walked through the restaurant door, lasted five seconds and said, "I'd be delighted." Then I drove home, literally sweating because I'm hopeless; scared stiff.'

Clarkson, afraid? This side of Jeremy, never revealed before, continued to make itself felt. Indeed, he appeared to be positively revelling in doing what he dreaded. 'I won't do after-dinner speaking because I'm terrified of that sort of thing,' he said. 'The idea of driving to Carlisle to entertain a load of drunken double-glazing salesmen on a Tuesday night, who may or may not throw things at me, fills me with fear and dread. It's easier to send the children up chimneys if you need a few quid.'

So why, he was asked, was he doing it? 'Men are just ego covered in skin and they were massaging it and saying, "Oh, you'd be so good,"' Jeremy said. 'And I'm sitting there thinking, "Oh well, I must do it then." I've been quietly pooing myself ever since I said I would, and I still am.' That might just have been overstating the case. Nerve-wracking it might be, but it was a phenomenal opportunity, all the same. Clarkson was going to be even more mainstream than ever before.

The new show presented another problem, too: this time a sartorial one. Jeremy's workaday uniform of jeans and a jacket just wasn't going to cut it here. At long last, he was going to be manoeuvred into a suit. Quite a few magazines had fun with this one, running spreads of him hamming it up in Savile Row's finest: a pro like him could hardly resist all the publicity that that one would bring.

But the image change could scarcely have been more startling – not just in the one-off shoots, but on screen when he hosted the show – and he wasn't much looking forward to the change, either. Smart clothes and Clarkson were not natural bedfellows, but a chat show host had to show he could cut the mustard and live up to the elegant image created by the likes of Michael Parkinson and myriad others, too.

'I don't know where you buy suits from,' he protested, before explaining that he had not necessarily been voted Britain's worst dressed man. 'Well, it might have been the second worst dressed man, which is even more embarrassing,' he added. 'All I'm concerned about is that, for the first time ever on TV, I'm going to be warm, instead of shivering on a hillside somewhere in Wales. I don't know what I'm going to do in a studio, but at least I won't be freezing.'

In the event, all was well-ish, and although the chat show never really took off, his popularity ensured it lasted for a few series. As for all this self-doubt: there's no question that Jeremy was nervous, but he did draw the critics' poison, as it were, before the show even began. If they thought he was awful when it aired – and some clearly did – well, Jeremy had already said he was going to be, and stated over and again that he expected the worst. In addition, the whole experiment made it quite clear just how highly Clarkson was regarded by the BBC.

CHAPTER 7

A SUDDEN CHANGE
OF GEAR

As the Clarksons shifted up a gear in the fast-paced life they were now living, the fact that Francie was Jeremy's manager was working increasingly well. She was a shrewd operator, quite aware of how famous her husband had become, quite aware of the full potential his profile now provided and determined that not only would he be paid properly but that he would also have the pick of projects that came his way. She made sure he was always prepared for everything, that his professional life ran as smoothly as his home life and that any potential problems were sorted out before they even appeared. She was, in fact, perfect for the role and has been a huge factor in her husband's massive success.

Jeremy himself is well aware of this and has paid fulsome tribute to her, and to the fact that she contributed as much to his career as he did. 'Francie is the human pinball operator and

I'm the ball,' he said. 'She just fires me off: she tells me what I have to do each day, the timings, what I have to wear, whether I need to shave, and she gives me a folder with a briefing of who I'm meeting and all the details. Without that I'd be completely lost.

'She's very tough in negotiations and I'm not. I'm just a pushover and say yes to everything. She hit the roof when she discovered I wasn't charging travelling expenses when I was driving all over the country. Now she checks the mileage on the car before I go and when I get back. I'm seen as the nice guy and she wears the hobnailed boots.' It is not an image his army of fans would entirely concur with.

Jeremy painted a good picture of her as the tough one, but Francie herself acknowledged that working as her husband's manager also helped keep the family together. It was practical: it gave her the feeling that she was working at her own career but, at the same time, meant she had time to be with the children — and, of course, her husband. The fact that they worked together meant that they didn't have to spend too much time apart.

But that had not initially been the plan. Just as Jeremy would often say the way his life turned out was really a matter of chance, so much the same applied to Francie. 'When I stopped work to have Emily, I had every intention of returning,' she said. 'I'd never had an idle day in my life, so while I was home, I helped sort out Jeremy's books and taking the phone calls. I knew that we'd have to find a good nanny when I went back to my job, because I'd be gone for twelve hours a day. The more I thought about it, the more I began to realise that we weren't going to be a family if I went back [to work]. I realised it wouldn't be fair on any of us and I'd be sacrificing a lot just for my job.'

It helped that she has the ideal personality for the role of a manager. Francie frequently paints a picture of herself as being a bit scatty but, in reality, she is straightforward, organised, efficient and determined. As she herself said, laziness is not part of her make-up, and so she didn't find it a problem to run both her husband's professional life and her home. She provided a good counterbalance to Clarkson's sometimes overenthusiastic nature: he might get carried away with his latest feud or his latest obsession, but Francie managed to keep her feet on the ground. And it speaks volumes for her that she stood out against such a strong personality as Jeremy. She might not be recognised in the street the way he is, but among the people who know them, she retained a personality that was just as strong as that of her famous other half.

And, of course, it helped that the two work so well together. 'I've found that being in business together works really well,' Francie said. 'If we hadn't, then we wouldn't have been so close, we simply wouldn't have had enough time together. When I read about Anthea Turner saying how much she was away and how it had damaged her marriage, it underlined that. I don't feel as if I've thrown anything away. I don't see myself as having made a sacrifice; this is another stage in my life. I like supporting Jeremy and being with the children. I'm probably perceived as living in his shadow, but he doesn't make me feel that way, he's very respectful of what I do. Someone said I'm Mrs Fifteen Percent, but they're wrong: I'm Mrs Fifty Percent; we share everything.'

It was not just work that the couple shared: it was their children, too. Family is actually very important to Jeremy, probably far more than most people realise, and so having Emily and Finlo was just as big a part of his life as his career. Asked if work occasionally dominated his relationship with Francie, Clarkson replied, 'We don't get a chance for that to happen because the children dominate work – we can't talk about it all the time. But it's very important that we have a marriage as well as a partnership. Working together, I know I can trust her implicitly, but I also love it when the kids come zooming into the office and interrupt me.'

He adores being a father. He would roughhouse with the children, and there were, after all, plenty of acres in which to play. And the children adore him, too: there was plenty of horsing around, playing and general silliness. Certainly, it was Francie who was the disciplinarian in the family: when the children were with their father, they wanted to have a laugh. And Clarkson was only too happy to provide it. This was the aspect of his life that no one ever saw, where he was not causing chaos, having to voice strongly held views or defend himself against whatever he had just said.

This kept him grounded and happy. It was, after all, the main point of his existence: a happy home life in which he could relax away from the public eye and be himself. It also showed the wisdom of moving out of London: because in the space of the Clarkson estate, the family could enjoy themselves without the fear of being watched. He taught all his children to drive almost as soon as they could walk – this is perfectly legal as long as it is on private ground – and indulged them with toys and countryside treats.

It was good for the children, too, to grow up out of town, in that it helped counteract their father's fame. Of course, Jeremy is as well known in the Cotswolds as he is everywhere else, but had the family been based in London, Emily and Finlo would have been much more aware of the status their father possessed. As it was, they were protected from some of the wilder excesses of fame – and, indeed, from some of its more negative aspects. Their father wasn't only famous, he was one of the most controversial men in the country and at least they have rarely witnessed the downside to that.

Above all, the estate provided a refuge for Clarkson. As his mother pointed out, it is exhausting to be Britain's most opinionated man 100 per cent of the time. Messing around with his wife and children, he didn't need to keep up the act. It isn't exactly an act, as such, for with Clarkson what you see is what you get, but even he needs time off and this is how he went about it. He and his family led a private existence, in contrast with the intensely public life he pursued the rest of the time. Living a peaceful, rural lifestyle, whatever he might say about heading back to London as often as possible, clearly kept Clarkson sane.

Having the support of his family behind him was also a big help to Jeremy when he went out to work in the wider world. And the new chat show was taking up a lot of his time: he had to stay in London during the week as work on the programme progressed, on top of which Francie had just discovered she was expecting again. Not for the first time, Clarkson came across as a naughty schoolboy trying to justify his actions.

'You just would not believe my behaviour,' he said, now resident part of the time in the flat the family had kept on in London. 'My wife's pregnant and looking after two small children and is living out there in the swamps. So I was very careful, my first week down here, to make sure that when I talked to her I said I'd worked late, cracked a takeaway and was in bed early … It was a great story and it was working brilliantly – until she got my credit card bills. Every night there was another restaurant. I've just been running around, injecting myself with a bit of London joie de vivre, which is great. It's magnificent to be back. When I'm old with my teeth falling out, I'm sure the countryside will be great, quite calming.'

Of course, in reality, Jeremy had something beside the new programme to think about. He was quite as excited about having another child as Francie, and could scarcely contain himself before the next baby arrived. 'We know it's a girl because we've seen the scan,' he said. 'Unless it's a boy with a very small … I don't know how she [Francie] puts up with me. She can't watch the news with me because I shout and scream and yell at everything and say, "I'd sort that out in ten minutes." So she leaves the room. But she's caring and kind and just rolls her eyes at my raving views on things.' Another daughter, Katya, duly arrived.

Whatever excitement there might have been on the domestic front, though, he remained the showman he had always been. Back at work, as the date for the new chat show to air drew near, Clarkson became increasingly animated on the subject he was to discuss. 'And can you smoke while scuba diving?' asked Jeremy, by way of an example of the kind of questions he intended to ask. 'It's an important issue and we have to address it. I'll never be able to keep my mouth shut, I know I won't. If someone says cricket is interesting, I won't be able to sit there and say, "Yeah, you're right," because it isn't interesting. I'll go, "Sorry, it's not, and it's time to stop it."'

As to whether his strong opinions would make him a good chat show host, Clarkson appeared to be having an attack of the vapours here, too. 'If you're as opinionated as I am, you're bound to alienate half the people half the time – or everybody all the time,' he said anxiously. 'I might have stones thrown at me afterwards! I'll probably have to go and live in another country until people have forgotten it.'

But that country would not be the United States. Unexpectedly, for the States is exactly the kind of place you would have thought would appeal to a man like Jeremy, he didn't like it, although he was quite clear as to why. 'I used to like America very much, until I went there,' he said. 'It drives me absolutely potty. They make a law for everything. It's illegal to shoot a tin of food in Idaho and you can't keep a pet alligator in Florida! Who would want to? I was once told to uncross my legs for take-off on an American airline. Why? If I hit the ground at 600mph, the positioning of my legs is going to have no bearing on whether I live or die.'

Of course, there was no real chance of Jeremy leaving the country and anyway, if his new show did fail, he still had the backing of his family. Both he and Francie seemed to appreciate one another more as the years went by, although she could be quite wry about the new status now afforded him. 'If we'd met now, we would never have been together,' she said. 'I would have been put off by his position and I'm quite sure that Jeremy would have been more cautious. When you have enjoyed the sort of success he's enjoyed, people treat you very differently and he'd wonder why I was there. I see how girls flirt with him. We call them the ironing-board girls because they're so slim and they're all fluttering their eyelashes and smiling. I don't feel jealous – why should I? Actually, I find it rather flattering to think I'm with a man who's so much in demand.'

And anyway, his career, according to Jeremy, was something of a surprise. It had just come about by chance. 'I've never had any ambition – in fact, I've always felt that it was a waste of time,' he said. 'All this has happened quite by accident. But now I'm here, I work a seven-day week because this sort of job doesn't last very long and you've got to make hay while the sun shines. What I'm doing won't last for ever. In ten years' time, there'll be someone younger and cleverer doing it. I don't want to be kicking myself for not having taken full advantage of it all.'

As he took advantage of it, Jeremy continued to manage both self-deprecation and controversial opinions at the same time. Clarkson was fond of telling interviewers he drove at 100mph in the countryside and, asked whether he had a death wish, was adamant that this was not the case. 'I drive at or below the speed limit on motorways because you're likely to be caught and in towns and villages because it matters,' he said. 'I follow drivers who go 45mph along an open road and don't reduce speed in a village. I'd remove their licences and birch them in public.' But, he maintained, the speed limit should be increased to a minimum of 130mph on motorways. 'Then you'd really have to concentrate, whereas at 70mph you can talk on the phone, eat a cheese sandwich and nod off. Of course, if I was a cyclist living in Devon and wanting a quiet life, I'd find myself very offensive. Occasionally I meet *Guardian* or *Observer* readers who see me as the devil incarnate because I seem to champion speed and recklessness. If you express opinions, you're bound to polarise people. You can't please them all, and if you do, you're grey.'

And with that, he was back on the attack. The French? 'They eat garlic and the women don't shave under their arms.' The Spanish? 'They murder bulls and can't cook.' The Germans? 'Ready for another war.' Motorbike riders? 'I'm heterosexual and don't enjoy dressing in leather.' Environmentalists? 'If others want to save the planet, good luck to them. I'm too busy going to parties.' The Americans? 'As dim as TocH's [gaslights], they want to eliminate all risk through legislation. You can't smoke within 40ft of a Federal building, but you can own a helicopter gunship and fire live bullets. Their lack of worldliness drives me barking.' But he only did it to annoy because he knew it teases. 'The trouble is, if you make jokes about women or homosexuals, everyone says, "How can you?"' he said. 'But it's a free country, so say whatever you feel.'

And as long as he continued to describe cars as amusingly as he did, he could get away with it. Jeremy's descriptive powers certainly showed no sign of flagging. He continued his diatribe against BMWs, not mellowed one jot by the fact that Francie had one, while summing up the characters of a whole raft of other car owners, too. BMWs are owned by 'sporty and aggressive drivers. No one has ever been let out of a side turning by them. Saab owners are the nicest, going quietly about their business. Lotuses are fun in a breaky-down sort of way – the name stands for Lots Of Trouble Usually Serious. Volvos and Mercedes estates are for the suburban mummy, who can pull her headscarf further forward so she can barge her way through without seeing where she's going. Shogun drivers feel superior to ordinary Earthlings, although they're not robust cars. The E-type Jaguar is perhaps a sexual metaphor, but it's not as good as sex, that's for sure. Even bad sex is better.'

But for all Clarkson's ability to amuse and upset, he kept his feet on the ground when it came to himself. He did not, as so many successful television presenters do, make the mistake of believing his own publicity. 'It could be done by anyone who can write scripts and is enthusiastic about cars,' he said of his work. 'Top Gear is half an hour of entertainment fluff on a Thursday night and it has no effect whatsoever. I was very rude about the Escort, which is Britain's bestselling car, and the world's bestselling Toyota Corolla.

'If you want passion, and I do, then it's the seven-headed beast from Revelations, boring as a washing machine, designed on a fag pack in the coffee break. It's probably the "We Hate Jeremy Clarkson" club at work. I don't mind people writing to tell me I'm stupid or ill-informed, but I wouldn't like to come face-to-face with them. I'm a bit shy, really.' It was not a self-assessment everyone would have agreed with.

Nor did Jeremy ever let up. He had by now made it into the august pages of *Who's Who*, where he listed his hobby as 'smoking'. He maintained his son's first word was 'Ferrari' and explained that 'to argue that a car is simply a means of conveyance is like arguing that Blenheim Palace is simply a house.' He even, of all extraordinary things, became the focus of attention because of the clothes he wore, and not in a complimentary way, either.

It was said that jeans had become unfashionable again, and that sales had fallen by thirteen per cent because people were put off by men like Jeremy wearing them. It became known as the 'Clarkson Effect', and Jeremy tackled it in his usual inimitable fashion. He had, he explained, got into trouble before: though Repton disputes it, he had been expelled from school; had the people of Norfolk found a 'We Hate Jeremy Clarkson' club; upset the makers of the Vauxhall Vectra; and called the Koreans dog-eaters. But now things had got serious. He was accused of having a deleterious effect on jeans.

'I once popped into town wearing a pair of jeans and, within five minutes, Falmers – a British jeans company – went bust,' he said. 'And now, Levi Strauss is set to close down half of its American factories. Six thousand workers will be made redundant. There'll be rioting on the streets; the National Guard will be called out.

'And, apparently, it's all my fault. Fashion gurus say that young people don't want to be associated with "old gits" like me and blame a catastrophic thirteen per cent fall in jeans' sales in what's been christened the "Jeremy Clarkson Effect". This is fantastic. Most people strive all their lives to get a miserable OBE or a so-what knighthood. And without even trying, I get my own "effect".'

★ ★ ★

All told, matters were chugging on in a pretty satisfactory manner when, at the beginning of 1999, Jeremy dropped a bombshell. He was leaving *Top Gear*.

The news was a shock to everyone. Jeremy Clarkson, who had single-handedly turned motor journalism into a spectator sport, was leaving the show that had made him famous. Could this really be true? So closely was Clarkson linked with the programme that had made his name – indeed, the suggestion had been put forward, quite seriously, that it should be called *Jeremy Clarkson's Top Gear* – that it seemed quite inconceivable that he would want to go. But he had been on the show for the best part of a decade and, like so many people before him, quite simply felt in need of a new challenge. He had been doing the same thing for a long time now and he wanted a break.

Jeremy was not going to be the only one affected by this decision. For a start, there were his fans. While Clarkson had not quite attained the status of a national institution, he wasn't that far off, and for all the people he upset, riled and insulted, he had an enormous fan base of admirers, too. They were inconsolable: Clarkson was their icon. A man seemingly afraid of nothing and no one, who was never worried about speaking his mind; a man whose twin obsessions were sex and cars. There was no one else quite like Jeremy on the national stage, and while he had no intention of leaving it − there was plenty still to be working on in the pipeline − he was the absolute personification of man's obsession with his car. Without him, could *Top Gear* continue as a programme in the way it had done before?

Not only was the public taken aback; it was a dreadful blow to the show's producers, too. When Jeremy had first started working on *Top Gear* nine years earlier, its viewers numbered in the hundreds of thousands. Now there were about six million of them and that increase was almost certainly solely down to Clarkson. While the other presenters were popular, no one had quite the same mix of sardonic humour and ability to ruffle feathers as Clarkson. There was, quite simply, no one else who could step into his shoes.

But why, why, why was he going? Jeremy was straightforward about it. 'I'd taken *Top Gear* as far as I could,' he said. That was how he felt at the time – he was later to change his mind and anyway, he now had so much else to preoccupy him. Not only was he doing massive numbers of other shows about fast-moving vehicles, but he was also a talk show host. Just where was he going to find the time to do *Top Gear*?

Clarkson himself enlarged on the subject: *Top Gear* was becoming ever so slightly predictable. He couldn't resist, however, putting it in his own inimitable way. 'I got out partly because it is based in Birmingham and Birmingham is terrible,' he announced. 'But I also found I was writing in a formulaic way. The personality became more important than the product, and that was hopeless. I did try to broaden it. I'd liken cars to potatoes or espresso coffee or something, but people would write in and say, "Talk about Claudia Schiffer's knickers", so I'd go back to those similes. By the end, I don't think I could have brought that programme another ounce of worth.'

So what was he going to do now? He was certainly much in demand. One group of people who clearly wanted him to find the time for them was the Conservative Party. Jeremy had never come down for one party or the other, but it would have been a little unlikely had he suddenly stood up and proclaimed his support for Labour, and so, initially, the Tories must have thought they were on to a good thing. More than that, Clarkson had recently pronounced on John Prescott's transport policy – 'His bill is lavatory paper in Phoney Tony's downstairs loo' – which would seem to indicate support for the other party. Wrong.

The row began when Francis Maude, the Shadow Chancellor, invited Jeremy to come and meet some senior members of the Conservative Party. He then went on to say: 'Jeremy has great insight into the motoring industry. We would be interested in getting together.'

If this was a clumsy attempt to latch on to some of Clarkson's popularity, it backfired spectacularly. Jeremy erupted, announcing he was going to 'drive to London to shoot whoever thought up this ridiculous idea. Working for Mr Hague would be the last thing I would do.' That was just the start of it. 'They have not been in touch,' he fumed. 'I do not have an invitation on my mantelpiece. I would not mind so much had Francis Maude actually written to me, but he hasn't. I have not had any form of communication. If a letter turns up, I will reply: "Thank you very much for your kind offer, but no thanks. I am not a politician."'

He became increasingly heated as he went on. 'I cannot remember ever having been so angry,' he snapped. 'I am no Tory puppet. When I heard what was being said, I said to my wife, "What did he say? What did this bastard say?" Their idea that I would want to get affiliated is barking. It is a magnificent figment of their imagination. I am not even slightly interested in party politics. The idea of working on behalf of the Conservative Party is ridiculous. They should be doing the job themselves.'

And, quite rightly, given that he had upset or insulted at least half the population on one occasion or another, he rather felt that he wouldn't be an ideal party spokesman in this age of spin. What about his calls for an upper speed limit of 130mph or his assertion that Korean car-makers eat dogs? 'No spin doctor would allow me to go on saying things like that, and I simply cannot help myself,' he said. 'I will not meet them; I do not have time. I don't know what is going to keep me busy, but I certainly do not have time to meet them.' Later, Jeremy complained in his own inimitable fashion that this was the first time a story had been utterly and completely made up about him – and what did it say? That he was the Tories' unofficial transport spokesman.

Not that Labour had much chance of signing him up, either: Jeremy disliked them even more. 'I'm not keen on politicians either – people like Prescott,' he said. 'No matter how daft my ideas might be, Prescott's are much, much more stupid. His ideas are just lard. He's the biggest, fattest waste of space in the known universe. Come the revolution, he's first against the wall. Because he's an idiot.'

But he certainly wasn't resting on his laurels. One aspect of Clarkson that has often been underestimated is quite what a workaholic he is. Because he comes across as so laid-back, it is easy to forget that he writes all his own material, including both his television work and the numerous commitments he now had on newspapers. He is aware of this, and maintains that he's good value, too. 'I do work very hard, massively so,' he said in 1999.

'There are three columns a week to write, and I have just signed a three-year contract with the BBC. I'm good and cheap. The megabucks deals are for people who are on

TV every day. If I'm on a programme, I have to be completely engrossed in every detail. That means I can't do all the multi-million deals. I just like work and I don't like mowing the lawn or playing golf.' That hard-working ethos is a long way from the beer-drinking laddish image Clarkson so often projects.

Nonetheless, he wisely kept his feet on the ground. For all the many criticisms levelled at Clarkson, no one has ever accused him of getting carried away with himself, and he continues to wrong-foot the people who sought to do him down by getting in there first. 'I still haven't come to terms with success,' he said. 'It'll probably go away. My hair will fall out, my teeth will go yellow, people will get bored. I already have a big hole in my hair and a huge beer gut.'

As time passed, it seemed that at least one reason why Jeremy had decided to give up *Top Gear* was that he wanted to step away from his more laddish persona. 'Everyone thinks of me as being like that, but I'm thirty-nine, with three kids and a house in the country,' he said. 'The public perception of me has always been slightly removed from the rather conservative person who actually exists. We wear tweeds and go to drinks parties, and bring up our children properly – all very twee and lovely. But if I couldn't escape to London I'd go nuts.

'Country restaurants are terrible. I can't tell fish from chicken, but I hate all these non-smoking places with their pour-a-sauce-on-it food. We moved to the country for the kids, but Emily can't stand it. She likes the Harbour Club, the Hurlingham Club, Jermyn Street. Everyone calls her Tara Palmer-Clarkson.

The real Tara has promised to take her shopping, and I'm going to hold her to it. I don't care what the bill will be. It would be worth it just to see Tara taking her up and down Sloane Street, introducing her to all the latest fashions. Emily would think Tara was God.'

And secondly, the chat show had been a success. It was commissioned for a second series, which promptly produced an attack of nerves in its presenter to rival the first one. 'You should see me backstage beforehand,' said Jeremy. 'I am always surprised to discover where I have sweat glands. My mouth is like Niagara, my back like the Atlantic, and I find it horribly nerve-racking. I am useless at interviewing. Ask anyone at Pebble Mill. I am the world's worst interviewer. Every time I do a programme, my heart goes like a washing machine full of Wellingtons and I think, "Why am I putting myself through this?"' But put himself through it he did.

You can't keep a good lad down. For all his attempts to adopt a more grown-up persona, Clarkson couldn't help himself: he was the walking, talking lad personified. All his tastes were those of the lad, from the car he drove to the music he liked, even when he was showing his more sophisticated and adult side. Asked why he had such a shite taste in music, Jeremy replied, 'I don't think I have got a shite taste in music. I like the Doobie Brothers; they're a very good band. And Steely Dan – no one could say Steely Dan are shite. They are probably the greatest, most talented collection of musicians ever to be brought together. I like Supertramp too. Went to see them at the Albert Hall. Absolutely fantastic! Even if it's unfashionable to say so.

A SUDDEN CHANGE OF GEAR

But I don't give a fuck about that; I've never been too bothered about appearing uncool.'

It could have been his life philosophy.

CHAPTER 8

A REGULAR GUY

On the subject of his natural ability to annoy, Clarkson remained unrepentant. Asked why he continued to upset so many people, he replied, 'You may have a good point. Perhaps we shouldn't do gays. Those pressure groups are so touchy. But why don't people suspend their beliefs and find everything funny?'

He really was turned off by homosexuality. It is impossible to escape the conclusion that an awful lot of his likes and dislikes are worked up specifically to amuse, but his distaste for gays was undeniable. Asked if he developed those feelings because of any gay sex at boarding school, he replied, 'No, I'm probably like that because there wasn't any. As long as people do it in their bedrooms, fine. But I find it slightly repulsive, well, grotesque actually. Is that homophobia? I suppose it must be, mustn't it? I just don't want people doing that sort of thing to come near me. My view has always been that we are put on earth to procreate.'

He was as capable as anyone of making it all into a joke, though. Another bugbear had become homosexual cars, something Clarkson was only too happy to expand on. 'It's a car that's a bit weedy, a bit effeminate,' he explained. 'With gay wheels. Obviously, some cars are more homosexual than others. A Fiat X19 is a very homosexual car. It purports to be something it isn't. It thinks it's a Ferrari. But it isn't; it's queer. Actually, my own Ferrari has been described as homosexual by no less an authority than Steve Coogan. Because it's got these raspberry ripple seats. Well, it also has a very powerful engine, which discounts it from being homosexual. Mind you, I'd sooner hear it called homosexual than have it called a Fiat.'

Sometimes, however, the fuss caused by what he said was just plain silly. On one occasion, Jeremy remarked that paella was made from rice and whatever happened to be in your bin, and was promptly labelled as being racist on the front page of *The Independent*. Clarkson himself pointed out that this really was nonsense.

When he wasn't upsetting gays, Spanish chefs and readers of the Indy, though, he was ruffling feathers elsewhere. It made the news when, writing in *Top Gear* magazine, Clarkson called for the legalisation of drugs. 'Eighty per cent of crime is drug-related,' he argued (with some reason). 'No one breaks into your house because they need funds for music lessons. They break in because they need smack and crack. And I'm sorry: we've got to give it to them. Legalising drugs will bring the price down and cheaper drugs will mean less crime. It's as simple as that. To argue that we'll all become junkies is nonsense. You can buy drink, but we're not all alcoholics.'

That wasn't all. 'CCTV has driven teenagers out of the city centres, so they queue outside remote farmhouses, waiting for their turn to defecate on an heirloom,' he continued in the usual Clarksonesque style. 'And where are the police? Well, they know you're only after a crime number for insurance, so they're about forty miles away, trimming their moustaches to look good on next week's edition of Police. Stop. Kill. The police spend all their resources on JetRanger helicopters and sophisticated infrared cameras to get action-packed footage of car-azy motorists. And the Crown Prosecution Service? That's busy sorting out the video rights.'

This had exactly the effect anyone could have predicted: uproar. People were queuing up to denounce this latest outburst. The police were less than delighted: 'He's talking through his denims,' said Ian Westwood, vice-chairman of the Police Federation. 'Legalising drugs is not the answer and when it was tried it hasn't worked.'

Nor were anti-drug campaigners impressed. 'What a piece of deep thinking – beat crime by legalising it,' snorted Peter Stoker, director of the National Drug Prevention Association. 'He should stick to driving instead of getting into a skid over this. Any time I want advice on drugs now I'll go to a garage, not a medical expert.' Not for the first time, Clarkson had shown an ability to provoke – and refused point blank to be penitent about it. At any rate, he would have been perfectly justified in saying that he was merely joining in the national debate.

As for his own easy-going persona, he was adamant that it was not an act. 'I'm the sort of bloke who always gets the last parking meter outside Peter Jones,' he said. 'I have never been depressed, never been in a bad mood. I can't understand why people do it. With women, there are biological reasons, so that is fine. But I know men who can wake up in a bad mood for no reason at all. Why?'

And despite the attempt to step away from his laddish image, Clarkson still liked to put himself forward as a bit of a philistine. 'I do wish I knew a bit more about stuff, but I have a loathing of any book that doesn't have a swastika, a gun and a girl in a bikini on the cover,' he once remarked. Again, though, this was living up to the public image. A rather more thoughtful Clarkson clearly lay behind the scenes, a fact testified to by his success. By this stage in the game, Jeremy had been going strong for nearly a decade: at the time of writing, he's been at the top for nearly thirty years. In the fickle world of television and entertainment, you don't maintain a career like that without some considerable nous behind the scenes.

Despite the macho image, at this point in his life – which was to change a few years later – Clarkson maintained that he had almost never been in a violent situation and wouldn't know what to do if he was. Fighter? Not him – or at least, only when he was pushed into it, something the erstwhile *Mirror* editor Piers Morgan might have had something to say about a few years later.

'I've never been in a fight,' he said. 'Except once, when I head-butted a bloke – the only person I've ever met who was taller than me. And I only head-butted him out of terror. I was out in America, doing a bit of skiing. We were discussing divorce, and this man's girlfriend said something I took exception to. I told her she was talking out of her hymen. So he grabbed me by the lapels and thrust me against the wall. He was 6ft 7in, this guy; fucking massive. I thought, "Oh my God, I'm going to be killed, I'd better get the first punch in." But other than that I've always avoided fisticuffs.' Clarkson was clearly a pacifist at heart.

Jeremy might not have been a fighter, but he was a very good sport. He was by now good friends with his fellow *Sunday Times* columnist AA Gill, a man who was as accomplished as Clarkson when it came to upsetting other people. And so Jeremy allowed himself to become the subject of articles written by his friend (he would repay the favour shortly) and, on one memorable occasion, accompanied Gill to Cheshire. Both gave their take on the trip, with very amusing results.

'For a place where the showroom is a cathedral of pilgrimage and the double garage a family chapel, Clarkson is the Second Coming,' Adrian Gill wrote. 'People don't mob him so much as genuflect to him.' Clarkson took it in very good part, not least when Gill, while commenting on the number of people who asked him for his autograph, kept whispering to the locals that Jeremy was actually gay; a little leitmotif that ran through the piece.

Indeed, Adrian and Jeremy had some fun ribbing one another. Gill made it clear that Clarkson was by far the more famous of the two, while at the same time teasing Jeremy on any grounds he could think of. After some slight ribaldry at the expense of the Cheshire set's obsession with nouveau-riche conservatories, lean-tos, ironwork and so on, he quotes Clarkson as saying, 'You know, it's worrying. Some of that stuff looked a bit like the stuff I've got at home – only a bit, mind.'

He was the butt of some more teasing when Adrian suggested they visit Wilmslow, the epicentre of the Cheshire set. 'I don't want to go,' Clarkson, whom Gill was by now calling 'Mr 0–60', announced. 'You go – they'll only point at me and tell me about their Porsches and what I said about their Cherokees.' In the event he did, of course, go along, and, according to Gill, was asked to autograph the thighs of various local girls in mascara. 'Can you put, "To a 911 driver with love?"'

They completed their weekend with a session on the golf course, which neither had tried before and both sneakily enjoyed. Both agreed, however, that it was an embarrassing sport to admit to having liked. 'You know, I rather like it as well,' mused Jeremy. 'I could take this up, but then I'd have to pretend to the wife that I had a mistress to get away at the weekend and hide my kit at a friend's house.' And, on hearing that Gill was preparing to out Clarkson as a secret golfer, he continued, 'That's torn it; that's the end. I'd rather be thought a poof than a golfer.'

Jeremy, incidentally, also wrote a very funny piece about how he had found Cheshire: 'It's just like England, only there's no class system, just the haves and the haves-even-more. Cleaners, I suspect, are bussed in from Moss Side and then shot.'

His family life certainly seemed to be running as smoothly as ever. The Clarksons had been happily married for over five years, and had three children, living – whatever Jeremy might have said in his more bad-tempered moments – an idyllic life in the country. Clarkson valued it, too, and would come out with the usual mix of laddish humour and assertions that it was really Francie who ran the household to back it up. 'I live in the real world,' he said. 'I can see why people split up, but I hope I never do. Make the wife wear metal knickers, ha ha. I have never been sexist. Francie is very keen to pick me up if I try that on – she sends me to do the washing-up.'

Indeed, Jeremy could get quite carried away on the subject of his wife. Theirs was not a small household, and their way of life was a far cry from the early days of living in a small London flat. 'We've got eleven puppies, three children, Francie has me to manage, the builders are in on a major job, and she's just been on a classic car rally to Sicily and back,' Jeremy said. 'Plus, she recently took the kids to Norfolk for a week, and put a big charity thing together. I don't know how she does it. She is unbelievable at coping. It is an old-fashioned marriage. And now I come to think about it, she does get the bum steer. All I ever do is work all weekend. I do nothing around the house, although I do spend as much time as I can with the children.'

He was growing increasingly wealthy too. Not that he boasted about that aspect of his life: Clarkson actually played down any idea that he was now one of the rich elite; it was probably a good tactic. Asked how many millions he was worth, he replied, 'One – that's about the sum of it: one. The million

I'm closest to is one. That's not to say I'm worth a million 'cos I'm not. No fucking way! But people see me on the telly and they think, "He's fucking minted; he must have his own Lear jet." Complete bollocks. You'd be amazed to know how little I got paid for *Top Gear*.'

That last point was almost certainly true. For a start, it was a BBC programme, and the Beeb is far from being one of the best payers in the land. Secondly, of course, while Jeremy was now a major star that had not been the case when he first started out. In fact, he was a complete unknown when he started on the programme that made his name, and his salary would have reflected it. It is only as time went on and his profile grew that Jeremy really began to have some money to play around with – and even then, as he'd be the first to remind anyone, in the grand scheme of things it wasn't a huge amount. He was certainly nowhere near super-rich.

Nor would he do absolutely anything to become a member of that particular elite. Asked once if he would ever pose naked, he replied, 'Quite simply, there isn't enough money in the world. I wouldn't care if Bill Gates offered me a thousand million. I wouldn't do it. I wouldn't eat my own shit and I wouldn't pose with no clothes on. I can't imagine there'd be much demand for photos of my hairy arse, either. Apart from a few mad old women, perhaps.'

And while Clarkson might not have been presenting *Top Gear* anymore, his career was going as well as ever. His latest programme was to be called *Clarkson's Car Years*, his producers quite clearly having decided that getting their star's name in the title was a good selling point. No sooner had filming started than there was a graphic illustration of the power of the motors involved: one of the production staff lost control of a £140,000 Lamborghini Diablo to be featured in the programme. It was actually a miracle no one was killed or badly injured as the car careered out of control just after leaving the car park, ploughing across two lanes of traffic in the centre of London before ending up smashed against a crash barrier in London's Park Lane. Jeremy was not amused.

'I'm absolutely furious,' he said. 'He's cost us a whole day and we're on an incredibly tight schedule. I warned the guy to be careful because the Diablo is an animal of a car, but he clearly didn't listen.' He then took a slightly calmer line. 'Perhaps he can be excused because the Diablo is like no other car I've ever driven,' he went on. 'Diablo means devil and, believe me, there's hellfire and brimstone under that bonnet. The sheer power must have given him the shock of his life; I'll bet he's still shaking.' The BBC itself was forgiving, deciding not to name the guilty party even though their insurance had to pay for the repairs. 'It was a straightforward motor accident. We are not identifying the member of staff involved,' said a spokesman.

Another aspect of work was his continuing mateyness with Adrian Gill. The two were friends outside of work, but continued to form a sort of double act professionally as well. Their Cheshire jaunt had been such a success that the duo next set off on an assignment to Iceland – a favourite haunt of Jeremy's – where more larks ensued. A typical snapshot of the shenanigans was this: 'Things were going quite well until about four in the morning when the two girls we'd picked up started snogging each other and our photographer was punched in the face ...'

There was a good deal more on these lines, eliciting the tart comment from the journalist and commentator Julie Burchill that the two of them were acting their shoe sizes rather than their age. Still, it made for a good read, not least because Francie, too, contributed a short piece, revealing Clarkson's long-standing obsession with Iceland was such that he had managed to be there not just when she gave birth to their first child – but when the dog had puppies, too.

There was a very small hiccup in his domestic life at this point in 2000, one that was ultimately going to lead to a massive feud with the then-*Daily Mirror* editor Piers Morgan. Jeremy, who had just turned forty, was snapped holding hands with and kissing Elaine Bedell, the producer of *Clarkson*, prompting a certain amount of speculation as to the exact nature of their friendship and an enraged riposte from Clarkson.

'I am not having an affair,' he snapped. 'We are work colleagues who were just fooling around.' His family also rallied around, with Francie expressing some exasperation about the shots. 'The paparazzi are a constant nuisance,' she said. 'They take photographs out of context and then print them. I phoned friends in case they thought we were parting, but most knew it wasn't true.' It was an experience that shook everyone, though. Clarkson was known to be a family man and nothing like this had ever been said about him before.

Rather more seriously, Clarkson was then blamed for the end of the production of Vectras at Luton. In one way, it was a backhanded compliment: it made it clear just how influential Jeremy was in the car industry, even if he himself continued to deny it. For the first time it emerged that, after a slot on *Top Gear* some years earlier that was unbelievably critical even by his standards – a lot of silent musing, followed by remarks that the car was boring and unworthy and that the only positive thing worth a mention was a device for removing tyre valve caps without getting your hands dirty – workers at Vauxhall staged a walkout, demanding to be told why something that could have affected their livelihoods was being treated as if it didn't matter. Some people might say that they had a point. 'We are concerned the BBC trivialised one of the most important entries into the British car market,' is what a Vauxhall executive said at the time.

But now Vauxhall was to stop producing Vectras in Britain altogether, although the car itself was still going strong. 'The Vectra is, and will continue to be, very significant for us,' said a Vauxhall statement. And, indeed, it was not going out of production altogether, merely in Britain. The factories in Germany and Belgium were still to continue producing the car.

It is hard to know what to say about Clarkson's role in all of this. On the one hand, his comments must have had some effect on the Vectra's fortunes: people did listen to what he had to say, no matter how much he may have played down his own influence. And it was a fair comment to say that he had perhaps placed too much emphasis on entertaining his audience, and not enough on the better qualities of the car, without realising what the impact of this would be.

On the other hand, it is not Clarkson's job to look out for the interests of the motor industry. And the fact that he is prepared to be irreverent and to tell it straight to the audience is one of his enormous strengths. The man himself, needless to say, was completely unrepentant about his role in the affair and refused to retract his comments; it could be argued that if a major car manufacturer could be damaged by the remarks of just one man, no matter how much weight his words carried, then they must also accept some of the responsibility for their product's fate. But it was a sad little episode and one that left no one involved looking their best.

People often wonder whether there is a darker side to Jeremy, one that broods blackly under all the cheery bonhomie. He may be considerably cannier than he lets on, but as far as anyone can tell, the answer is no. With Clarkson, very unusually in the world of celebrity, what you see really is what you get. And it has stood him in good stead too. He has never seemed overawed by the world in which he now moves, has never let himself get carried away with it and refuses to give in to resentment and bad humour. It is just not him.

'Well, if I have a philosophy, it's this: get born, live your life, die,' he said. 'And don't worry about anything in between because it's a waste of time. My attitude is that if I get up in the morning and I'm still breathing, I'm quids in. You get people who worry about the ozone and stuff like that. But look out the window: it's all green and clean. What's the problem? I just can't see it. I hardly ever worry. I don't suffer from depression, I don't even have moods – if you're in a bad mood, you're wasting time.'

This was also an attitude that he was keen to pass on to his children. 'When I was growing up, we laughed at every calamity that struck,' he said. 'Now I tell my kids, laughing is the most important thing. You fall over. Laugh. Someone's nasty to you. Laugh. Life is short and you haven't time to be stuck in traffic jams or be sad.'

It was an approach to life that was confirmed by his wife. The only time Jeremy was not on form was when work had been particularly onerous, she said, not because he was in a foul mood. 'Surprisingly, he doesn't have mood swings, but there are times when he is tired or preoccupied and not quite so much fun,' she explained. 'But he is never stroppy for no reason – unlike me, which happens every twenty-eight days or so, he claims.' Some women, of course, would have risen to this one, but Francie knew her husband too well. She simply ignored it and got on with things. Indeed, if she hadn't been able to, the marriage might not have worked as long it did: of all the qualities Clarkson needed in a partner, tolerance came very high up the list.

However, even Jeremy had a softer side. He might have denied it, but just occasionally he could be wounded by something someone said – although he would be the first to accept that if you dish it out, you also have to be able to take it. He thus practically never complains publicly about anything anyone says or does (apart from the irritation he expressed about people begrudging him his Ferrari), and so it fell to none other than his mother to let on that Clarkson was actually more susceptible to criticism than he has us believe.

'People might find this hard to believe, but he does actually get hurt by some of the things people say about him,' his mother Shirley revealed. 'He'd never let on, though. It's as if he feels he's got his laddish image to live up to. To be honest, I don't think he enjoys having to keep up the image twenty-four hours a day. Like if he's taking Francie and the kids out for a meal, there might be someone having a go at him for slagging off their car and he feels he has to join in the fun and be "Jeremy Clarkson from the telly". He thinks it's too dangerous to show people his softer side.'

But, as Shirley was the first to concede, it was down to the way he had been brought up. 'All the Clarksons are like that,' she confessed. 'We deal with emotions by having a laugh. It was this rather jolly approach to life that allowed him to make what appeared to everyone else to be outrageous decisions and then express surprise that anyone else was upset. One such occasion occurred early in 2001, when Clarkson decided to buy a 60ft long Lightning jet fighter, which had been made in 1960 – the year of his birth – and decommissioned in 1988, and put it in his front garden. His neighbours promptly complained.

'My wife Francie hasn't spoken to me for two days since it arrived,' said Jeremy, as he confessed it was just a wee bit bigger than he had been expecting. 'But I love the thing. It is a seriously impressive piece of machinery and is much, much better than a water feature in the front garden. I must confess it looks a lot bigger here than at the airfield where I first set eyes on it, but I think it's great. The complaints have come because, although I have a fairly big front garden, the plane is so huge you can see it above the hedges. Sadly, the engines have been removed because it would be very handy to have used it to clear up fallen leaves and other garden litter. It's also exactly the same age as me – and I plan to keep it exactly where it is.'

He got a little bit more irritable about his new toy as time wore on. Disclosing that he paid less for it than the price of a Ford Fiesta, he continued, 'The council were around after three minutes, but we're not overlooked so I can't see what the problem is. I thought we won the war, didn't we? We're in talks with the council. Apparently it's a grey area of the planning law. But my children love it. They use it as a giant climbing frame and it's lovely to look out on first thing in the morning. And it's definitely better than having gnomes on the lawn.'

Could this irritability stem from the fact that he sometimes had problems sleeping? Clarkson did, after all, have an extremely active life and it would be no surprise to discover that the stress did sometimes take its toll. He was slightly grumpy about this too. 'The worst thing about insomnia is that no one else sympathises,' he announced. 'Tell anyone you can't sleep and they'll give you chapter and verse on how easily they nod off. When I meet a blind person, I don't tell him I can see just fine.'

There was another brief hiccup around this time: after three series, the chat show had been cancelled. Clarkson had done a perfectly good job, but it had never really taken off in a big way and he sounded faintly relieved to be out of it. 'It wasn't my thing,' he explained. 'The first series was pretty awful and I was getting better, but I prefer being outdoors in a pair of jeans.' On another occasion, he remarked, 'It's very difficult to do that kind of show because there are so many. There were some very good guests. AA Gill was good; he didn't mind making a fool of himself on television.'

And with that he was off to make his next television programme, this one called, quite simply, *Speed*. His TV career as a whole was going as strongly as ever and, as ever, the label of the new programme was true to what you got in the tin. Clarkson was pitched at colossal speed in any number of situations, from jet fighters to rollercoaster rides. For the latter, he enlisted an unusual companion: his mother.

'We wanted to do a test on The Big One roller coaster at Blackpool Pleasure Beach,' said Jeremy, 'and I thought, "Who can I get to do this? I know, I'll get my mum." Of course, she hated the idea and she hated the whole experience, but I bunged her £100 and she was OK with that.'

Indeed, the trials Clarkson was about to put himself through were, if anything, even worse than those in *Extreme Machines*. Nor was Francie thrilled that her husband was risking his neck yet again. 'I assured her that I'd never do anything like that again,' he admitted. 'Unfortunately, this producer friend of mine from school phoned me up with a wonderful idea to do a lot of things very fast and I couldn't refuse him. I don't suppose Francie was too happy about it, but she's got used to me saying and doing my own thing over the years.'

Jeremy's willingness to put himself through it was commendable. He was also exceedingly willing to talk about just how frightening it had been. 'I know that half the people tuning into *Speed* will be doing so just to see me make a fool of

Top: Jeremy Clarkson as a young boy, age nine.

Bottom: A very unusual road-test: Clarkson trying out Tesco's new supermarket trolley in a west London branch in 1997.

Top left: Clarkson and Piers Morgan are all smiles before the champagne kicks in on the last commercial Concorde flight from JFK to Heathrow. © *REX/Shutterstock*

Top right: Clarkson with his former wife Frances and their three children at the London premiere of *Johnny English* in Leicester Square.

© *Justin Goff/UK Press via Getty Images*

Bottom: Clarkson, James May and Richard Hammond posing with one of the many awards that *Top Gear* picked up as it became the one of the world's most popular TV shows. © *Dave M. Benett/Getty Images*

Top: Clarkson trying to beat the horde of paparazzi on his trail after he was dropped by the BBC following the 'fracas' with *Top Gear* producer Oisin Tymon.

© *Justin Tallis/AFP/Getty Images*

Bottom left: Appearing with the man who was to briefly take his place as *Top Gear* host, Chris Evans, on his Radio 2 show in May 2015.   © *SAV/GC Images*

Bottom right: Up to their usual tricks: Clarkson and Hammond during their arena tour, styled as 'Clarkson, Hammond and May Live!' as a result of their exit from *Top Gear*, in Sydney in July 2015.   © *Matt Jelonek/Getty Images*

Filming of *The Grand Tour* took Clarkson, May and Hammond around the world. From Australia to Italy, they drew huge crowds (and caused a scene) wherever they went. *Top © Mark Metcalfe/REX/Shutterstock; bottom © Awakening/GC Images*

myself and they won't be disappointed,' he said. 'We had a series of disasters and I've never been as genuinely frightened as I was doing this. Up to now I thought nothing would faze me. How wrong I was. People have been killed going down bobsleigh runs and when I asked if I was insured, people just laughed at me. Then, about halfway down, doing 80mph, the serotonin in my brain kicked in and I froze with fear. It's what causes rabbits to freeze in front of car headlights. I couldn't move – all I could do was grunt. After the run they wanted me to comment on how I felt, but I couldn't speak.'

Jeremy also very sportingly found himself being sick in a cockpit again, this time courtesy of the Empire Test School in Wiltshire. 'It turns out that *Top Gun* is for pussies,' he said. 'If you're a good Top Gun instructor, then you end up at this place in Wiltshire where they do this manoeuvre that no one else in the world teaches you.' The manoeuvre in question was certainly not for the faint hearted. 'I was taken up to 42,000ft and then they stall the engine, so you go into freefall,' Clarkson explained. 'You fall axis over axis and I was explosively sick everywhere. I felt dreadful and I was in a fair amount of pain. I didn't feel much better when we landed either, or for about three days afterwards, and I really don't want to repeat the experience.'

He did, however, enjoy it on the whole. 'I also met some incredibly interesting people,' he said. 'I crashed Colin McRae's rally car and I raced an extreme skier down a red ski run in Austria in a baby Jag, which was hair-raising. You had to stay above 80 miles an hour otherwise you get bogged down. The course was about five miles long, but it was almost vertical in places. It was fantastic. Hopefully, a lot of viewers will tune in because they are interested in how and why we go faster and how fast we'll go in the future. But I also know there will be people watching who hate me and are only waiting to see me suffer. There are plenty of those, believe me.'

CHAPTER 9

BACK TO THE FUTURE

A s Jeremy's career became increasingly successful, his leisure pursuits were expanding. Clarkson had taken up shooting, explaining, 'I have decided that the best thing to do with the view is to eat it.' This, perhaps, explained his sympathy towards Prince Charles, whom he praised in typically flamboyant style: 'Now Prince Charles has shown himself not only to be a decent cove, but also the kind of leader this country needs,' he announced. 'Unlike John Major, he obviously has rather more than two pubic hairs in his underpants.'

And on the work front, the Jeremy and Adrian show was flourishing. The two were now taking regular jaunts to various destinations together, all reported on with much jocularity in the pages of *The Sunday Times Magazine*. The expeditions made extremely entertaining reading, not least because the two sturdy travellers were prepared to poke a great deal of fun at themselves, coming across more like two excitable schoolboys than members of the great and good.

'We've been to America, Iceland and Mykonos,' crowed Clarkson. 'We've also been up the M1, visiting everywhere with a brown sign to see if they really are of interest. Adrian got excited, but then all he knows is South Kensington and the Ivy, so to him a caravan site is strangely thrilling.'

He was still enjoying being a grumpy old man, though. Asked what he considered to be the worst thing about driving in Britain, he replied, 'Speed cameras. I could sit here and come up with a million things, like old men with big ears in J–reg Rovers who drive too slowly, but the proliferation of cameras really annoys me. When they first came along, and were going to be put in blackspots outside schools and be visible so you'd be forced to slow down, they were a good idea. Now there are 6,000 of them, none of which appears to be in accident blackspots, just hidden behind bushes; [they made] £71 million quid last year, from 6 million people being caught. That's 10 per cent of the population criminalised, more than a quarter of the motoring population. Most of them were little old ladies doing 32mph.'

But he had not lost his sense of humour. Clarkson was still eminently capable of laughing at himself: when asked, as a motoring enthusiast, whether he had leather driving gloves, aviator sunglasses or a Genesis album, he replied, 'I have the gloves and, furthermore, the index finger and the middle finger on the right hand are red, so you can make highly visible V signs. Sadly, I don't have aviators. I used to own a pair in 1978, but only Robert Redford can wear them. And no, I don't own a Genesis album – I own all of them.'

And that self-same sense of humour continued to get him into trouble. The RSPCA felt moved to issue him with a warning after he announced one day that he had just been hunting rats using tennis rackets and croquet mallets, something for which he remained entirely unrepentant. Indeed, he also raised eyebrows when he revealed how to smoke on airplanes: 'I don't smoke nearly as much now, but yes,' he said. 'You kneel on the pump thing to keep the vacuum going in the toilets, to get rid of the smoke. It's very undignified, but I was never caught.'

And, as usual, the targets of his jokes never realised he was not always being serious. It is very unlikely that Jeremy would have employed a tennis racket to track down a rat and, as for smoking in the toilets of planes – well, even if he had done it, as he himself said, it was hardly the most distinguished image to create in the readers' minds. Sometimes it almost seemed as if he couldn't help himself – if it was going to upset people, he said it – and at others, it was almost as if he took a delight in jarring delicate sensibilities. But either way, as with the naughty child Clarkson so often resembled, the trick was not to rise to it, something that time and again people forgot.

Indeed, at times it seemed as though the disapprovers were out in force. Yet another was Transport 2000, which called for *Top Gear* to be replaced with a programme that was more safety and environmentally aware. Indeed, they were merely the latest in a string of organisations to do so. For years, environmental protestors had been having a go at *Top*

Gear and in Jeremy, of course, they found the perfect target to complain about, for the simple reason he was so very politically incorrect. Another presenter might have tried to play down the environmental issues a motoring programme will inevitably come up against: for Clarkson, however, the confrontational approach seemed best.

The feud with Vauxhall was also still going strong. In an attempt to prove a Vauxhall could be driven from the back seat, Clarkson did exactly that and crashed. Asked where he was when he crashed, he replied, 'In the back seat.' On yet another occasion, during the Top Gear Car of the Year Awards, he dumped nearly half a ton of manure on a Vauxhall van. Sometimes, of course, these ploys seemed rather childish, but they still delighted viewers.

However, that reference to not smoking so much, made on the subject of smoking in planes' lavatories, was a sure sign that age was beginning to catch up with even the mighty Clarkson. Many people absolutely revel in smoking in their youth, but once on the wrong side of forty, it starts to seem like not such a good idea. And it wasn't just his own health he had to worry about: he had his children to look after, too. Jeremy would have denied it, but these days he was taking slightly better care of himself. Not that he had the slightest intention of slowing down.

Nor was there any indication that anyone would want him to. Since 1996 he had released a motoring video annually, a profitable venture that was still going strong. He was also now writing a series of books, which went on to become bestsellers.

Ever more interesting television programmes were coming his way – of which more in the next chapter – home life was happy and his life was an interesting one. These days he merely realised that to continue to get the maximum out of life, he would have to look after himself a bit better.

But there really were indications now that he was feeling his age. He once wrote that, in his youth, he and his friends left a restaurant either when they had run out of money or when it [the restaurant] had run out of wine. Now they went home because they were tired. On the whole, however, he was coping well with middle age. Life had, after all, turned out very differently from what he and his parents had feared when he was younger: he was, and still is, one of the best known faces in the country and all for doing a job that he loved. His current position in British society would have seemed inconceivable in the dark months after he had been 'expelled' from Repton, and, indeed, in the happy lad-about-town days of his youth. Clarkson had never, after all, gone out to make a career for himself in television: his really was a career that had started by pure chance.

Even better work was just around the corner. Clarkson had done plenty of non-car-related television already, but he was about to show a far more educated and cultured side to himself than many people could have believed existed. On top of that, he retained his fan base of lads, who loved everything he did and wanted to be like him. As his appeal broadened, so did the range and number of projects he came to be associated with. It turned into a virtuous circle: as Clarkson became more popular, more work came his way, which made him even more popular. And, by now, it was perfectly possible to have seen a huge amount of Jeremy Clarkson on the television without seeing him go anywhere near a car.

And now he was back, bigger, bolder and better than ever before in the show that had originally made his name. Not that he'd exactly been away from television altogether, of course: his presence on our television screens was almost as frequent as that of *The News At Ten*, but he was returning to the programme that had made him famous: in 2002, less than three years after leaving, he was back with *Top Gear*. And, to be honest, they'd missed each other. The programme hadn't been the same without him, while Jeremy himself, although kept busy, had not found a permanent replacement for his first true amore. And so he was going back, in a move welcomed by his television bosses and fans alike.

But it was not just that Clarkson was returning to *Top Gear*: the programme itself was undergoing a complete transformation. Everything was to be new: some of the old presenters had gone off to Channel Five, while the show itself had been taken off air for a year while BBC executives pondered its fate. That they saw its best hope for the future in a presenter who had left three years previously says a great deal about Jeremy's role in making the show the success it had been: if it was going to be must-see TV again, they wanted him back. And then some.

Their man was only too happy to oblige. Jeremy might not have been making the programme any more, but his love of cars was still as strong as ever, and he was only too happy to get back into the driving seat. He was also only too happy to offer his take on the challenge of reforming the show. 'The old *Top Gear* was too formulaic,' he said. 'Every day I was filming miles away from home, getting back late and writing the next day's script.

'One night, I had a Renault Clio to review and I couldn't think of a single thing to say. All those little cars were fine; all economical, all could do 100mph, all had cup-holders. What I wanted to write was, "Want one? Then buy one. Don't want one? Then don't." Instead, the cursor on the screen winked at me until 2am and I knew I'd reached the end of that particular road. But I still loved cars. I had an idea for a new show just when the other presenters buggered off to Channel Five, so here we are. But this time it's studio-based and we have our own test track so we can drive fast and talk cars – I want to make talking enthusiastically about cars less embarrassing than it is at the moment.'

One inspiration for this, no one should be surprised to hear, was Clarkson's old friend AA Gill. 'You know, I knock around a fair bit with Adrian Gill and people come up to him all the time and coo, "Oh Adrian ... restaurants ... where do we go? How can we get a table? What's the latest thing to drizzle over sun-dried tomatoes?"' Jeremy said. 'But if anyone wants to talk to me about cars, they do it in hushed tones in case anyone hears. I want to change that.'

Quite a few changes were being made to the format of the show. It had been extended to an hour and considerably sharpened up. 'The programme will be topical because it's made just a few days before it's screened,' Clarkson explained. 'I'll also be very picky about which cars get on the show; if a car isn't special and different, it won't get seen.'

It also gave him a chance to go back to doing what he liked best: racing very fast cars around without worrying about besmirching his licence. Jeremy's proud boast remained that, while he didn't have so much as a point to his name for any driving offences, he was able to behave recklessly in the course of doing his job. 'I went to Japan to try the Daihatsu Charade and, after only half a lap, I had a huge crash and stuffed it into a ditch,' he said.

'Luckily I was wearing a helmet that punched a hole in the windscreen and I was fine. I was going too fast. I've also crashed a Jaguar XJR 15, worth £750,000, and I recently drove a Ford RS200 into a ploughed field. It's the fastest accelerating car in the world – it does 0–100mph in six seconds, too fast for me, but I'll have a go at anything. I particularly like driving fast when I'm taking a corner, it's quite a sexy feeling.' Off duty, though, it was a different matter. 'I'm very wary,' said Clarkson. 'I've never been flashed by a speed camera.'

He also couldn't resist the odd dig at the old crowd he had previously worked with on *Top Gear*. Asked if motoring ever got tedious, he replied, 'Not for me. It's great fun. Since we changed *Top Gear*, I don't have to drive the boring cars. People say, "I'm thinking of buying a Renault Clio, what's it like?" I haven't got a clue; I've no idea. Watch Channel Five, I'm sure they'll tell you.'

But it wasn't just the programme that had changed; Clarkson had, too. He had mellowed somewhat, something he was keen to put across to the public, and even claimed that he was no longer out to cause upset just for the sake of it. 'I'm forty-two, and when I did *Meet the Neighbours* [a programme in which he travelled around Europe comparing the stereotypes to the reality], I was much more gentle,' he said. 'Now, with *Top Gear*, I'm being billed as, "bigger, bolder and ruder than ever before", but to be honest, I'll only court controversy when I think it's worth it, not for the sake of it.'

A Jeremy Clarkson not deliberately stirring it up is much like fish and chips without the chips – one vital ingredient is missing – but that wasn't all. He was showing a softer, more vulnerable side, even admitting that his feelings could be bruised. Asked if it hurt when people slagged him off, he replied, 'Yes, it does. But I dole it out so I have to take it. Now, if I was David Attenborough and someone was rude about me when all I'd said was, "Look at these lovely meerkats", then that would be unfair. Or if I was Alan Titchmarsh talking about a nice cotoneaster and someone called me a tosser, then I'd have every right to moan. But I take a car that someone's worked on for five years and call it rubbish. That's hurtful, so I can't complain.' In that he was right, but he was certainly proving he knew the score.

He was still merrily dishing it out left, right and centre. The Germans remained a favourite target, even as far as their attitude to the English is concerned. 'They still think that everyone in Britain is either a squadron leader or a Brontë sister,' Clarkson announced. 'We go to work with tightly rolled umbrellas and bowler hats. We only eat food when it's charcoal and we only ever watch films about the war.'

Or take this one about another old favourite, Norfolk. 'The government should stop promoting the Broads as a tourist attraction and should advise visitors that, "Here be witches,"' he announced. 'They spend millions telling us that it's foolish to smoke, but not a penny telling us not to go to Norfolk – unless you like orgies and the ritual slaying of farmyard animals.'

Or this, on a new target: footballers. 'I found myself sharing a hotel with a team that, thanks to the libel laws, shall be nameless,' he said. 'But honestly, the lobby was like Darwin's waiting room.' With that kind of savage wit it is hardly surprising that he had to take a dose of his own medicine from time to time.

As part of the new, gentler Clarkson (which, it must be said, never entirely materialised), the Ferrari was gone, to be replaced by a Mercedes SL 55, although, as usual, he tempered praise with a good deal of criticism. Asked what was the best car he'd ever owned, he replied, 'The one I've got now. It's a Merc SL, but it does break down often. Mercedes have completely lost the plot. They announced a few years ago they thought they were over-engineering their cars and were going to back off a bit in terms of quality, and it's showing. The dealers are rubbish, too. I know they're having a major overhaul, but they need to get it done in the next six or seven minutes.'

But he still liked to put himself forward as a man in touch with his gentler side. He was caught – openly – with flowers. 'You should see what I just bought,' he beamed. 'Two huge bunches of dried flowers. They're so big we can't get into the sitting room, but I don't care because they look great.' Even so, he retained a very sharp tongue when necessary: to date, he has been the chairman of the BBC's *Have I Got News For You* twelve times – not a job for the unwary.

This new, gentler image was rather undermined as Clarkson embarked on an enthusiastic explanation of his next project: his contribution to a new programme called *Great Britons*. It purported to find out who was the greatest of them all, with various personalities putting the case for all of them forward. The full list was as follows: Brunel, Churchill, Cromwell, Darwin, Princess Diana, Elizabeth I, John Lennon, Admiral Lord Nelson, Sir Isaac Newton and Shakespeare.

Clarkson's choice was Isambard Kingdom Brunel, and it soon turned out that he was taking his task seriously. Indeed, he sounded almost passionate as he put forward his man. 'He built modern Britain and, as modern Britain built the world, Brunel built the world,' he said. 'He built the railways, docks, bridges, harbours and dug the first tunnel under the Thames. He was a brave man. As for other contenders, Shakespeare brought misery to the classroom. Churchill was a drunk in the right place at the right time, Darwin was a plagiarist and Oliver Cromwell a communist. And as for John Lennon – "I am the egg man?" – I don't think so.' So much for his gentler, more caring side.

Brunel, who lived from 1806 to 1859, was in many ways an obvious choice for such a dedicated lover of boys' toys as Clarkson. Born in Portsmouth to a French engineer father, he was educated in Hove and the Paris-based college Henri Quatre, before returning to Britain, where he was involved in some of the greatest engineering projects of the day. In 1838 he designed the Great Western steamship, which was the world's largest vessel until 1899, as well as many of Britain's most famous docks, including Bristol, Cardiff, Monkwearmouth and Milford Haven. He designed the Clifton Suspension Bridge, which was completed after his death, to say nothing of a huge network of tunnels, bridges and viaducts for the Great Western Railway.

Clarkson's choice was certainly approved of by other Brunel fans. 'You only have to look around you to see the lasting impact he still has on us today,' said Mike Rowland of the Clifton Suspension Bridge Visitor Centre. 'If you travel by rail from Bristol to London, you see his work all around you and then there's the huge effect he had on the infrastructure of the city docks. His broad gauge was actually more efficient and safe, but it was discarded – wrongly in my view. Also, not many people know that, during the Crimean War, he helped Florence Nightingale by helping to design and support a pre-fabricated hospital for the injured.'

It was a very astute choice for Jeremy to make. His championing of Brunel changed the public perception of Clarkson as it became apparent he was a lot more cultured and erudite than he'd ever let on. There was no talk of twanging knicker elastic here: his appreciation of Brunel's work showed a genuine architectural aesthetic, as well as an admiration for how much Brunel had achieved. '[We can learn from] his sheer capacity for work; the volume was quite immense,' Jeremy said.

'From the whole of the rail network around the south-east of England, through India and Italy, tunnels in Bath, bridges in Bristol, Cornwall and Scotland, railway buildings such as Paddington Station. The other thing is he built things which last. I see buildings thrown up now in London, and I think, "That looks nice, but it won't be here in 100 years." When Brunel built something, he built it to last for ever.'

But Clarkson was Clarkson, and he was simply incapable of writing about or talking about anything without adding a slice of controversy to the mix. Writing about the colossal leap forward in the post-Industrial Revolution nineteenth century, he continued, 'But then we arrived in, ooh, about 1920 and everything just stopped; mobile phones; word processors; the Eurofighter … They're all just developments of ideas that came along in the nineteenth century. And it's easy to see what went wrong: the British Empire collapsed.'

Clarkson got into his stride. Brunel might have been a genius, but it was Empire and entrepreneurial spirit that allowed him to achieve what he did. 'I'm going to use Isambard Kingdom Brunel here as a case study,' he went on. 'When he fancied the idea of building a new train or a new bridge, or a new tunnel, he had to find benefactors. And they were everywhere, gorged with cash from the Empire's 11.5 million square miles and its 400 million inhabitants. Initial estimates for his Great Western Railway, which was to link London with Bristol, suggested it would cost £2.8 million. But this, as things turned out, would only have got it as far as Slough. The actual cost was a truly astronomical £6.5 million.

'And when it was finished he went back to the financiers and said, "Let's keep going. Let's take the passengers off the trains in Bristol and put them on steamships to America." And they agreed, paying for the SS *Great Western* and then the SS *Great*

Britain and, when that ran aground, the enormous SS *Great Eastern*, the biggest ship the world had seen – or would see – until the *Lusitania* came along fifty years later. Now imagine if IKB were around today. And try to imagine how far he'd get if he suggested to Network South East that it should finance an idea he'd had for scramjet flight to the space station and then plasma drive rockets to the most distant of Saturn's moons.'

He was equally effusive on screen. Typical of his way of putting Brunel forward is this: 'And the extraordinary thing is that a modern propeller, designed by a computer in the twenty-first century, is only 5 per cent more efficient than this propeller [on the SS *Great Britain*], which was designed by a Victorian bloke in a tall hat … the guy was a genius!'

It is not putting it too strongly to say that Clarkson single-handedly changed the public perception of Brunel. Until then, he (Brunel) had been thought of, in as much as the majority of the public thought of him at all, as a distant and little-known engineer from long ago, who possibly had something to do with bridges. After Clarkson's impassioned championship of the great engineer, public knowledge of what he had achieved shot up to such an extent that he actually came second in the final run-up, losing out only to Churchill.

Clarkson was not surprised by the outcome – 'As soon as I saw Winston Churchill on the list, I knew he was going to win,' he said. But what was amazing was that a figure about whom so little had been previously known among the public ranked so high. No one could have forecast this. Whatever his detractors might have thought, this was all down to Clarkson.

This new side to his character meant that people began to take him a lot more seriously. The city of Bristol launched a bid to become the European Capital of Culture in 2008, and started to put together plans for an international festival in 2006, Brunel 200, to celebrate the bicentenary of the great engineer's birth: Clarkson was one of the most high-profile backers. Again, it gave him the opportunity to talk about Brunel in the most glowing tones, and to expand upon why he really had been such a great man.

'Darwin told us where we came from, but it was Brunel who took us to where we wanted to go,' he said, sounding almost lyrical. 'He deserves to be fêted for his genius and vision, and Brunel 200 will be a wonderful way of showing everyone why he must be regarded as our Greatest Briton.'

It was a prestigious project with which to be associated. 'Brunel 200 is a key element in our cultural planning over the next decade and has all the makings of a marvellous festival,' said Andrew Kelly, head of the Bristol Cultural Development Partnership, who was also involved with getting Bristol shortlisted as the European City of Culture.

'At one level, it is a celebration of the wonders of the Victorian age – steam railways, ships, bridges and bold architecture. At another, it provides an opportunity for serious examination of the role and status of engineering in the twenty-first century. Brunel would be delighted that Bristol retains its reputation for exciting and innovative engineering through the Airbus wing design centre at Filton. The A380 super-jumbo is certainly in the Brunellian tradition.'

Back in his normal world, the Clarkson bandwagon rumbled on. The new, revamped *Top Gear* was doing well, his popularity as high as ever and Jeremy as boisterous as ever. His new, gentler side had disappeared again and his opinions were in no danger of becoming any less stringent: 'It seems that teenagers are leaving school these days well versed in the dangers of Ecstasy, but with no real idea of how to spell it,' was one barbed remark.

As far as his own children were concerned, now they were growing up. By the time their father returned to the programme that had made his name, Emily was eight, Finlo six and Katya four. It was in his youngest child that Jeremy saw himself best. 'It worries me a great deal,' he confided. 'She is stubborn, full of beans and ignores you if you don't say what she wants to hear. She's also very tall and has curly hair, like me. They are my playmates. If I'm left in sole charge, they won't go to bed on time and they won't have a bath, but they will graze their knees and fall over. We go and race go-karts around the fields together and they love it – I just want to have fun with them.'

He couldn't resist introducing controversy even into the subject of his children – although he had his limits: motorbikes were a no-go area. 'They might take drugs at some point, although I'll be pleased if they don't, but if any of them goes near a bike, I shall put a match in the petrol tank and set fire to it,' he announced. 'They are noisy and dangerous.'

Given this attitude, it was interesting that none other than Francie had just passed her motorcycling test and was the proud owner of a Honda 125. 'I passed the test at the second attempt,' she revealed. 'But I won't be taking anyone out as a pillion passenger because I think it is too dangerous. I don't mind putting myself at risk, but I don't think it is fair to put others in danger.'

It was as if, in the presence of such a strong personality as Jeremy, Francie sometimes felt the need to assert her own individuality. And Clarkson himself was adamant that it was Francie, not him, who ruled the roost. He relished the fact that she was his manager, as well as running the home, as it gave them yet more in common. 'It means she feels involved in what I'm doing, otherwise it would be easy to lead separate lives as I'm away filming such a lot,' Clarkson said. 'I respect her views: if she says, "Don't wear that," I won't wear it; if she says, "Don't say that," I won't say it. I honestly have no idea why she loves me. In fact, sometimes I can see the hatred in her eyes. She rolls her eyes at things I write and says, "You know it will get you into trouble, don't you?"'

But it would be a miracle if he didn't land in hot water, given his lengthy career as an irritant. And Jeremy thoroughly enjoyed his image, for all the talk of hurt feelings and calming down. If he didn't, he would, after all, have changed tack, whereas he was well aware that calling Churchill a drunk who was in the right place at the right time was hardly going to go down as one of the less controversial statements of the day. But that, of course, is why he is so good at what he does. Viewers do not tune in to Clarkson for mild-mannered patter: they turn the TV on to get attitude. And he rarely fails to come up with the goods. But now he had proved he had depth as well. He may well have been a motormouth, but that's not to say he wasn't exceedingly capable of flexing his intellect.

CHAPTER 10

CLARKSON STRIDES OUT

The programme about Brunel was not the only thoughtful piece of broadcasting Clarkson did around this time. He also presented a documentary of the history of the Victoria Cross, a stunning programme in which he followed the story of Major Robert Henry Cain, who had been awarded the Victoria Cross for gallantry during Operation Market Garden in September 1944. Again, the programme showed that Clarkson was far more than just a laddish TV presenter with a passion for cars: he came across as thoughtful, mature and appreciative of the deep sacrifices made by the men who had fought so valiantly for their country.

The subject matter meant that he was branching out more and more. He clearly adored being back on *Top Gear*, but it was, by a long shot, no longer the most important part of his television career. There was, in fact, quite a bit to choose from these days, from serious documentaries to larking around in shows like *Extreme Machines*, *Waterworld* and all the rest. But this new show was clearly a product of his more serious side. Perhaps Clarkson had tired of being seen as a buffoon in so many eyes and wanted to prove he could also be as erudite as the next man.

In order to bring the story of the Victoria Cross to life, he decided to focus on one story, that of Major Cain, to illustrate quite how brave the men awarded the medal had been. It was a successful and intelligent way of getting the facts across, for it was a moving story and one that the free online encyclopedia, Wikipedia, summarises as follows:

Robert Cain was born of Manx parents in Shanghai, China, on the 2 January 1909, and worked for Shell in Thailand, and later Malaya, until the war began when, in 1940, he was commissioned into the Royal Northumberland Fusiliers. He was later posted to the Second South Staffords and participated in the glider assault on Sicily. Commanding B Company, the thirty-five-year-old major flew to Arnhem with the First Lift, travelling in a Horsa from Manston. However, they had only been airborne for five minutes when the tow rope became disconnected from the Albermarle tug, causing the glider to stagger while the tow rope coiled up and lashed back at them. The glider made a safe landing in a field, bumping over the rough ground and ripping through a fence before coming to a standstill. Cain described it as a terrible anti-climax, and said how the glider pilot couldn't believe his luck, as exactly the same thing had happened to him on D–Day.

Cain and his men flew out to Arnhem as part of the Second Lift on the following day. Upon landing, he immediately set out to find B Company, who were presently moving forward to help the First Para Brigade, but he wasn't able to resume command until late on the following morning, when they were involved in vicious fighting in a dell around the area of the St Elizabeth Hospital. The South Staffords were being heavily attacked by tank and self-propelled guns, but they weren't able to bring up any anti-tank guns to repel them. Mortars were effectively being fired at point-blank range upon German infantry, but the Staffords had to rely on PIATs to deal with the armour. Lieutenant Georges Dupenois kept several tanks at bay with his PIAT, while Major Jock Buchanan and Cain drew a lot of enemy fire by running around searching for ammunition for him. Cain did not believe that any tanks were actually disabled during the action, but the hits did encourage them to withdraw; even firing at the turrets when Bren guns forced them to move. The PIAT ammunition ran dry at 11.30am, and from then on the tanks had free reign over the area and proceeded to blow the defenceless troopers out of the buildings they occupied. Lt-Colonel McCardie came to see Major Cain and he ordered him to withdraw from the dell. As they were talking, Cain recalled seeing an entire bush being blown clean out of the ground. Putting down a rear guard of about a dozen men and a Bren gun, the Company withdrew from what Cain later described as the South Staffords' Waterloo. However, only himself and a handful of other men succeeded in escaping.

Falling back through the 11th Battalion, Major Cain informed them that the tanks were on their way and requested they give him a PIAT, though sadly they had none to spare. He withdrew his men beyond the Battalion and gathered all the remaining South Staffords under his command. Though C Company was largely intact, at this stage he only managed to form two platoons from the entire battalion.

As the 11th Battalion were preparing to capture some high ground to pave the way for an attack by the rest of the Division, Lt-Colonel George Lea decided to utilise Major Cain and his men by ordering them to capture the nearby high ground, known as De Brink, to lend support to their own attack. This they did, but were soon spotted and came under very heavy mortar fire. The ground was too hard for the men to dig in and so they took many casualties. After he saw the destruction of the 11th Battalion, Cain took the decision to withdraw his men, numbering only 100, towards Oosterbeek.

Cain appeared to have developed an intense loathing of tanks after the bitter experiences of his Battalion on Tuesday, 19th, and he personally saw to it that as many were destroyed as possible. If ever armour approached, then he would grab the nearest PIAT and set out to deal with it himself. On one occasion, two Tiger tanks approached the South Staffords' position, and Cain lay in wait in a slit trench while Lieutenant Ian Meikle of the Light Regiment gave him bearings from a house above him. The first tank fired at the house and killed Meikle, while the chimney collapsed and almost fell on top of Major Cain. He still held his position until it was 100 yards away, whereupon he fired at it. The tank immediately returned fire with its machine gun and wounded Cain, who took refuge in a nearby shed from where he fired another round, which exploded beneath the tank and disabled it. The crew abandoned the vehicle, but all were gunned down as they bailed out. Cain fired at the second tank, but the bomb was faulty and exploded directly in front of him. It blew him off his feet and left him blind with metal fragments in his blackened face. As his men dragged him off, Cain recalls yelling like a hooligan and calling for somebody to get hold of the PIAT and deal with the tank. One of the Light Regiment's 75mm guns was brought forward and it blew the tank apart.

Half an hour later though, Cain's sight returned and, against doctor's advice, he refused to stay with the wounded and declared himself fit for duty. He also refused morphia (which was in very short supply) to ease the pain he had. Instead, he armed himself with another PIAT and went in search of tanks, frequently alone. Tigers continued to harass the Lonsdale Force and, upon hearing that one was in the area, Major Cain raced out to an anti-tank gun and began to drag it into position. A gunner saw him and ran over to assist, and the two men succeeded in disabling it. Cain wanted to fire another shot to make sure that it was finished off, but the gunner informed him that the blast had destroyed the gun's recoil mechanism and it could no longer fire.

On Friday, 22nd, his eardrums burst from his constant firing, but he continued to take on any tanks he encountered, contenting himself with merely stuffing pieces of field dressing into his ears. Nevertheless, he never ceased to urge his men on and was seen by his driver, Private Grainger, giving a man his last cigarette.

Monday, 25th, saw very heavy fighting in the area occupied by the Lonsdale Force. Self-propelled guns, flame-thrower tanks and infantry took great interest in Cain's position. By this time there were no more PIATs available to the major. Undeterred, he armed himself with a 2in mortar and added further trophies to his collection, while his brilliant leadership ensured that the South Staffords gave no ground and drove the enemy off in complete disorder. By the end of the battle, Cain had been responsible for the destruction, or disabling of, six tanks as well as a number of self-propelled guns.

As the Division was about to withdraw, some men were encouraged to shave before crossing the river: they were determined to leave looking like British soldiers. Robert found a razor and some water and proceeded to remove a week's growth of beard from his face, drying himself on his filthy, bloodstained Denison smock. His effort was noticed by Brigadier Hicks who remarked, 'Well, there's one officer, at least, who's shaved.' Cain happily replied that he had been well brought up.

Major Cain's conduct throughout was of the highest order, both in terms of personal actions and leadership ability, and for this he was awarded the Victoria Cross, the highest and most prestigious award for gallantry in the face of the enemy that can be awarded to British and Commonwealth forces; he was the only man to receive this medal at Arnhem and live to tell the tale. His citation said of him: 'His coolness and courage under incessant fire could not be surpassed.' He is buried in Sussex. There is a chapel in the Hospice at Douglas, on the Isle of Man, that is dedicated to his memory, and also a memorial scholarship at King William's College. The Staffordshire Regimental Museum holds several items relating to the major, including his Victoria Cross and the Denison smock and maroon beret he wore at Arnhem.

When the programme went out, it caused something of a sensation. Ever since his championship of Brunel, it had been clear that Jeremy was a far more thoughtful and intelligent man than he was usually given credit for, and here was more proof still. This was recent history, intelligently conveyed to the masses, with no horsing around, pontificating or giving in to specific prejudices. It was, to put it another way, grown-up television, aimed at a very different audience from the lads who doted on

Top Gear – although, because of Jeremy's involvement, it would have attracted them too.

And in true theatrical style, Clarkson held one bit of information until the end, for it was only then that he revealed that he was married to Major Cain's daughter, Francie – and that she had not known that her father, who died in 1978, had received the award. It had never occurred to him to tell her and it was only because her husband uncovered the story that Francie discovered what a hero her father had been. It is one of the most successful pieces of broadcasting that Clarkson has done to date.

Of course, Clarkson maintained plenty of other interests, among them a new show called MPH '03, billed as a motor show with a difference. 'Motor shows are pretty much dead in this country,' said Jeremy, explaining the rationale. 'The notion of turning up and mooching around in a huge crowd, and occasionally catching a glimpse of a wheel of a car you could see outside anyway seems a bit stupid. MPH '03 is where you can look at the more exciting cars on stands, but then there's a proper indoor racetrack to go in, sit down and watch cars going quickly. Cars are supposed to move, that's what they're meant to do. It's the future of motor shows. If we get round without a crash a day, I'll be astonished.

'I thought people would be interested in information, but no one gives a damn. Driving is supposed to be fun. Cars are a symbol of our release, our freedom, so enjoy them. Stop twittering on about the damage they do to the environment, and speed limits.'

And he was good-natured enough to appear on a special charity version of the BBC's *What Not To Wear*. Rather unusually, stylish presenters Trinny Woodall and Susannah Constantine actually appeared to have met their match: 'You look like you should be selling vegetables in a market,' they snapped, before being informed by Jeremy that, actually, he too hated the jeans-and-geography-teacher look. But he fought back. 'I'm not wearing a blue suit and a purple shirt,' he announced, before adding that it made him look like a photocopier salesman. 'I've never worn a jumper in my life,' he continued. 'People who wear jumpers are bullied.'

Indeed, on this occasion, the girls certainly weren't getting away with pushing their subject around. 'When I look at this wardrobe, I feel …' Trinny began. 'Moist?' Clarkson helpfully interjected. He then went on, 'I know this programme's all kind of … cushions … but I'm a man – I like fighter jets!' This led to another bout of national goodwill towards Clarkson: not only had he managed to take on two of the sharpest tongues in television and hold his own, but he had also come across as self-deprecating and modest. It was that old trick again – do yourself down before anyone else has the chance to. It works every time.

In fact, Jeremy thoroughly enjoyed the experience, no matter what he said. He certainly wouldn't let on, though. 'It was four days of utter abject misery,' he sighed. 'Every time I tried to go into a Bang & Olufsen shop, they'd drag me back out again. Trinny and Susannah were actually very sweet.' As to whether the experience made him want to be better dressed – well, no, not really. Asked if he thought he was uncool, Jeremy replied,

'No, I know I am, I just don't care; I live in the middle of the countryside. So long as you can't see my genitals, I consider myself to be well-dressed.' It was precisely the attitude you would expect from him.

Not that he was letting up on the aggro in other ways. On one of his favourite subjects – smoking – he was as cutting as ever, giving, as would be expected, very short shrift to suggestions that smokers should pay for their own health care. 'Smokers pay £19,000 a minute to the Exchequer and that's enough to pay for the whole police force,' he snapped. 'Or to put it another way, every £1 we cost the National Health Service, we give it £3.60. Please don't encourage the state to dictate how I live my life.'

He was also capable of ruffling feathers among the rural community. A newly converted country dweller Clarkson may have been, but that didn't stop him from expressing irritation about some country-dwelling habits. He caused yet another furore when he complained of the 'din' caused by church bell ringers, which stopped him from being able to have a Sunday lie-in. '[There are] bell ringers creeping out of their houses before dawn on Sunday mornings and using three tons of solid brass to wake us all up,' was his own, inimitable way of putting it.

This was a complaint that went down very badly with the people of Castor, a little village near Peterborough. It was home to none other than Jeremy's sister Joanna, and the villagers were sure that he was referring to the bells of St Kyneburgha's, the local church. Indeed, so indignant were they that one of the bell ringers, Tony Evans, felt moved to write to the *Parish News*. 'Clarkson promotes and enthuses over noisy, air polluting vehicles that race around our overcrowded country lanes and he is complaining about a custom that goes back over 1,000 years,' he snapped. 'I understand that he occasionally spends a weekend in Castor.'

Fellow parishioner Jenny Hammond was equally upset. 'Who does he think he is?' she asked. 'I'm furious he thinks he can come here and say these things. But I laughed when I read the piece in the parish magazine.'

The vicar, the Revd. William Burke, was more restrained. 'I think Mr Clarkson's comments were uncalled for, but he's entitled to his view,' he said. 'We will just have to learn to live and let live.'

But was he writing about the village at all? It is a mark of Clarkson's impact upon his readers that so many take so much so personally when it might actually have had nothing to do with them in the first place. Clarkson's sister, Joanna, was adamant that this was the case. 'Jeremy hasn't been here for a whole weekend and I don't think he's ever heard the bells,' she protested. 'He lives in rural Gloucestershire, so he could have been writing about there.'

That episode, small as it was, is actually a key to Jeremy's success. In whatever he says or does, he somehow manages to establish a direct connection with the viewer or reader, which makes it appear that a one-on-one conversation is going on. That is why so many people get so intensely het up about his views. Although they might know on an intellectual level that

Jeremy was pontificating in general, on an emotional level they felt he was talking directly to them. Thus they took what he was saying as a personal attack and responded in kind. On the other hand, when the reader or viewer agreed with him, they tended to feel an especially strong connection, which is why his fans can be so passionately in favour of his views and sympathetic to his irreverence and outspoken nature. It is as if he is their personal friend and champion in saying to the rest of the world what they themselves believe.

Indeed, he had actually become quite an advertisement for the joys of country living. The family had dogs, a range of cars, of course, and an exceptionally agreeable lifestyle. Clarkson knew it, too. 'Only last week I was at my children's sports day, and as I lay in the long grass by the river drinking pink champagne and chatting with other media parents, I remember thinking, "I love being middle class,"' he said. It was another quintessentially English scene that Clarkson adored being a part of.

Indeed, so established as part of the great and good had he become that there was even talk of him presenting a BBC documentary about Prince Charles. 'It's still very much in its early stages,' said a cautious BBC spokeswoman when the news emerged. 'Nothing is definite. It has not even been given the green light.' The idea was that the programme would look at Charles's work rather than his private life, and would in itself be a part of the Prince's search for a meaningful role for the modern monarchy.

'Royalty is highly contested in England and he cannot be immune to the fact that many people do not agree with the concept,' said Leon Krier, who had known the Prince for twenty years and had worked as his architectural advisor. 'He saw he could do more than take part in ceremonies, open buildings and smile. He saw he could have an influence and constitutional monarchy is justified and legitimised by his very attitudes. While politicians have a very short-term agenda, he can do things that take a generation to be proved right.'

Clarence House was circumspect. 'We continually look at ways in which to explain and illustrate the Prince of Wales' work and role, and that of his organisations and charities,' a spokesman said. Clarkson himself would not be drawn on his views.

And there were other aspects of his life, too. It is not often appreciated that both Clarksons do a fair bit of work for charity, particularly in their area of the Cotswolds. Home life was also very settled, not least because, for all his opinionated image, Clarkson was actually extremely easy to live with. There was only the odd blip, as Francie once revealed, shortly after that notorious garden ornament had finally been removed.

'The wackiest thing he ever brought home was a jet fighter, which ended up in our garden,' she said. 'Jeremy had always wanted a plane as a garden ornament. Before I knew it, it was being craned in. He's actually very easy to live with. He doesn't shout and rage. If something pisses him off, he just says it and gets it sorted. He does have an opinion on most topics, but he just says things that people think but don't dare say. He's a great dad and he tears around the paddock teaching the children to drive.'

His children certainly brought out Clarkson's best side. He

loved being a father and was good at it, too, as Francie had previously acknowledged. 'Jeremy is a brilliant, fun-loving father,' she said. 'I put this down to the Peter Pan principle, which enables him to build dens out of furniture and turn bath time into a scene from *The Poseidon Adventure*. But as a hands-on man, he's not so hot. I am sure he could do it, but he always seems to be in another country – and preferably another continent – wherever there's a whiff of nappy to be changed.'

It rather appeared that at home, at least, it was Francie who ruled the roost – even when it came to deciding which car the family would have. 'You might imagine that being married to the country's most opinionated motor writer, I would have little influence over car matters in our household,' she once wrote in the BBC's *Parenting* magazine. 'The reality is that I spend more time in our school-run car (a Volvo XC90) in a week than he spends in his own car in a month. And that lands me with the job of deciding which car we have.'

And the highly successful Jeremy and Adrian partnership continued. Both would routinely rope the other in to join in with whatever project they were working on, as, for example, when Gill took Clarkson to review a restaurant called Café Grand Prix in London's Berkeley Square. 'What would be the point of knowing Jeremy Clarkson (actually, what is the point?) if you couldn't take him to a dining room devoted to carbon monoxide and driving in circles,' he wrote.

And with that there followed the usual laddish jokes at one another's expense. Relating how they started off in the bar, which was decorated with photographs of famous racing drivers, Gill rather waspishly wrote, 'Jeremy walked round it squeaking, "Ooh look, here's Andy Di Pandyo, Daffy Di Duckyo and Tommy Di Jerryo, who were probably the …" and, in the gap while he prepared to drop a gear and tell us what they probably were, we escaped upstairs to the restaurant.' Gill was the perfect sparring partner for Clarkson: equally prepared to cause upset, equally dismissive of anything he didn't like, and prepared to poke fun not only at his friend but also at himself.

Back at the day job – *Top Gear* – Jeremy was thoroughly enjoying himself. One reason why he stuck with the programme for so long was that he clearly loved the fun involved in making it, and the interplay with his fellow presenters. Asked once what was the most fun he had had while driving a car, he replied, 'This morning came damn close, in the Noble with Richard Hammond behind me in a Morgan trying to keep up. That was as funny a thing as I've seen in a very long time. He was a speck in my rear-view mirror.' Of course, there was a genuine chemistry between all the presenters: they enjoyed one another's company and they enjoyed teasing each other too. The show was a happy one to work on, although it was not exactly a family atmosphere – more a group of men bonding over machines.

Clarkson was still managing to cause trouble in sleepy English villages wherever he went, although the next upset was inadvertent. It was, however, the latest in a series of mishaps: Jeremy had recently beached a £120,000 Bentley at Budleigh Salterton, Devon, while filming for *Top Gear* and, before that, while making one of his *No Limits* videos, had driven a Ford

RS200, the world's fastest production car, into a potato field in Fife. Now *Top Gear* had been staging a running gag: it was testing the durability of a Toyota pick-up truck. To this end, it was, among much else, submerged in the waves at Burnham-on-Sea in Somerset and, ultimately, perched on the top of a tower block before being dynamited. It made for good television and the viewers enjoyed it.

But, as one of the tests, it was driven into a chestnut tree in the little village of Churchill, north Somerset. The tree, rather unfortunately, was standing in the village graveyard. More unfortunately yet, while the Toyota proved its worth and escaped the encounter undamaged, the same could not be said for the tree, which was left with a gaping hole in the middle. This did not amuse the local villagers, and neither did the fact that the *Top Gear* team left without telling them about the damage improve matters. It was only when a villager saw the segment being broadcast that everyone finally worked out what had really happened to the tree.

'It was very mysterious and annoying,' said Pam Millward, deputy chairwoman of the council. 'The villagers think it's a bit of a cheek, just to come along and deliberately ram into a tree and drive away. At first, the BBC claimed they could not ask permission from anybody as it was such an isolated spot. But there is a notice nearby with names and contact details of myself and the vicar, so they can't have looked very hard. *Top Gear* is not my choice of viewing, anyway, but I do not think Mr Clarkson will be doing anything like this again.'

There was massive embarrassment at the BBC. For a start,

it could not be proven that Clarkson was actually the person behind the wheel of the car, but it was certainly a prank associated with him, something that probably strengthened the locals' complaints. Next, the BBC felt compelled both to apologise and to pay £250 in compensation. 'Top Gear has unreservedly apologised to the parish council for driving the pick-up into the tree,' said a spokeswoman. 'In acknowledgement of this, we have sent the parish council compensation – a donation for them to use as appropriate.' The council announced that it would go towards a new children's recreation ground.

It was not Top Gear's finest hour, nor that of the BBC. It was, however, so typical of the programme to go driving into trees, the reasoning went, that it was almost to be expected. And the BBC coughed up in the end and gave the village something to put the damage right. Clarkson himself regretted nothing. 'The parish council is funded by central government, which is funded by me, so it's my tree,' he said. 'Anyway, there was no damage.'

The stunt didn't lead him to lose any fans. In fact, he was gaining them and the lads who had always loved him, the devoted followers of Top Gear, his videos, books and other speed-related projects, continued to hero worship him. They were not going to turn against him, now. But he was also building up another following, one that was not interested in motor journalism but who did enjoy the documentaries he made. And Clarkson enjoyed making them, too. Having discovered something about Francie's family history, it was time to turn to the Clarksons themselves. Jeremy was about to embark on yet another serious documentary: one that would take him deep into his own family's past.

CHAPTER 11

WHO DO YOU THINK YOU ARE?

Jeremy Clarkson had come a long way. His television career had been something of an accident and, although he was perfectly competent for his first three years of reporting, he had not stood out. His real success only began in 1992 when, as he himself admitted, the production company encouraged him to speak his mind rather than to follow a polite script. The success of that tactic has resonated from that day to this, with the upshot that Clarkson is now one of the most successful media personalities in the country.

Instantly recognisable, for his distinctive appearance and deep voice have also helped him get a phenomenal amount of public recognition, Jeremy's career soared higher than anyone could have dreamt of. The truculent teenager 'expelled' from school had so far outshone most people of his generation that it is sometimes difficult to remember that they are the same person.

But the key to success in a career like Clarkson's is constant reinvention. Television is an unforgiving medium and what one day seems new and shocking shortly afterwards becomes clichéd and tired. No one who manages to maintain a long-term career on the box can afford to sit back and let newcomers catch up with them: they must maintain their edge and provide constant diversion for the viewer. And, wittingly or not, that is what Jeremy has done.

During the 1990s, when he was in his thirties, he was the personification of the lad. Rail against it he might have done, but it stood him in phenomenally good stead. It was the fashion of that moment, and Jeremy, with his liking for cars, booze and women, not necessarily in that order, appeared to sum up the whole feeling of the time in one man.

But what works in a thirty-something man can look a bit tragic a decade on, and so, with brilliant timing, the Clarkson persona underwent a change. Yes, there were still all those remarks about cars that snapped knicker elastic – old habits die hard – but now there was something more substantial there as well.

Jeremy had shown he had a far greater understanding of history, architecture, engineering and, indeed, of Empire, than anyone would have guessed, and it stood him in brilliantly good stead. It deprived his detractors of at least some of their ammunition, while adding a whole new layer to an already well-known personality. To paraphrase a cartoon of the 1980s, it showed he was deep, and not just macho. And, because of the massively more complex aura that now emanated from

Clarkson, it also widened considerably the range of work for which he was now suitable. In other words, it made him even more employable.

Now that the new, improved Clarkson had an altogether more serious image, it was almost inevitable that he would be included in the BBC's next big idea, a programme entitled *Who Do You Think You Are?* The show did exactly what it said on the label: it invited a number of celebrities to delve into their own backgrounds and find out where they really came from.

The idea worked on several levels: it sparked a countrywide interest in genealogy, as viewers were inspired to find out more about their own family tree, and it uprooted quite a number of interesting stories from the people who took part. Apart from Jeremy, they were naturalist Bill Oddie, actresses Amanda Redman and Sue Johnston, journalist and TV presenter Ian Hislop, newsreader Moira Stuart, comedian and author David Baddiel, soprano Lesley Garrett, actress and author Meera Syal and comedian Vic Reeves.

As it happens, Clarkson was not initially interested: 'Too boring to bother with,' he said, when first asked if he would like to find out more about his family's past. But the BBC persisted for good reason, for, as mentioned in the first chapter of this book, Clarkson had an interesting family background, in that his great-great grandfather had invented the Kilner jar. It was not just a popular television presenter they wanted to make use of: they also wanted someone with a real story to uncover and Clarkson was it. After some persuading, he finally agreed to take part, stating that he had a specific aim: 'Selfishly, I'm quite keen to find out what happened to the money,' he said. 'Is there somewhere a dusty piece of paper that says Jeremy Clarkson is owed £48 billion?'

With that he was off, displaying his usual mastery of the loaded question, the subtle pause and his not-inconsiderable skills as a broadcaster. Jeremy was already aware that one of his ancestors had invented the Kilner jar, but didn't know much more than that. His own parents had known that there had once been a great deal of money in the family, but that there wasn't anymore, possibly because it had never been registered in the first place. Whatever had happened, though, they knew one thing: the money had been lost.

Now Clarkson was intent on finding out the whole story. And, of course, Jeremy started his search for the truth in his own inimitable way. 'Take the Clarkson name back to its Yorkshire roots and they all come from within a few miles of each other,' he said. 'I'm the product of 200 years of interbreeding – I'm surprised I haven't got one eye!' But some of those Clarksons had been very pioneering indeed, playing a full role in the Industrial Revolution and making a fortune for themselves in the process. John Kilner established a number of glassworks in the north of England, among them the Providence Glassworks in Conisbrough, which became the main source of employment for the town. The family's importance can be judged by the fact that there is a Kilner bridge in Conisbrough, where the family also helped with funding for the local Methodist church.

Not that Jeremy had ever been particularly bothered about all that. 'I used not to care a tinker's cuss about my family past,'

Clarkson said. 'That there was this family tree, starting with me at the bottom and spreading back to the eighteenth century, and including 200 people, all of whom were born, lived and died within 12 miles of each other, struck me as spectacularly dull. But when I discovered they were part of British social history and the Industrial Revolution, rather than just part of my family tree – which is only of interest to me and my mother – I got involved.'

Given his earlier championing of Brunel as the greatest ever Briton, his family history could hardly have been more appropriate. Clarkson was probably the most well-known admirer of the nineteenth century and the Industrial Revolution in the country, and now it emerged that his own family had played a part in it. Had someone written out a plot beforehand, this would have been it: laddish television presenter shows his serious side by a piece of interesting and informed journalism about a great engineer at a time when Britain quite literally ruled the world – and then turns out to have had ancestors who also played a part in that glorious past. It built up interest in the programme, while at the same time establishing Clarkson as a far more in-depth character than he himself made out. Jeremy was now in real danger of turning into a national institution and this programme was yet another reason why that transformation was happening. He wasn't just mouthy; he had depth. Indeed, even people who had formerly loathed him were beginning to see the point of Clarkson. There was real affection in the way that many members of his audience regarded him now.

But, alas for Jeremy, the family money had disappeared long

ago. American glass-manufacturing methods became more popular than British ones, on top of which the vast family fortune was mismanaged, with the patent passing into other hands. Clarkson tracked down the current patent holder and cheerily remarked that he wanted to punch him, before calming down. 'It's just thrilling to know that my ancestors were part of the most extraordinary superpower the world has ever seen,' he said. 'Part of that patchwork quilt of ingenuity.'

But it was, perhaps, worth it just to have discovered his fascinating family history. And it wasn't just a tale about the Clarkson family: it was a story that somehow summed up a whole slice of British history – even mirroring the rise and then decline of the British Empire, not that Clarkson would have made such grandiose claims. But he did point out that it was a tale redolent of the times. 'The story is about the astonishing rise and calamitous fall of one of the many businesses that propelled the British Empire,' he said on another occasion, in the *Radio Times*, explaining the nub of what happened.

'My great-great-great grandfather John Kilner, who was born in 1792, had a glassworks that produced the Kilner jar, which is still used today for preserving fruit. The most amazing thing for me was discovering how big Kilner Glass was. I thought they made sweet little bottles in Doncaster, but it was one of 3,000 products, and the company had its own shipping fleet and railway sidings. When his son Caleb died, he left 120 houses along with lots of land in Bridlington. But the company went bankrupt! I'd come home after days digging around in Warwick library, wondering just how Kilner had got it so spectacularly wrong. It seems Caleb's son, George, just wanted to build churches and read the Bible, so he wasn't cut out for the gritty business of running a northern glass factory.'

The full story went something as follows. John Kilner had actually started out as an employee in a glass factory before deciding to go it alone. He enlisted the help and support of friends and, by the time of his death in 1857, had made the company enormously successful, owning two factories in south Yorkshire. After he died, the business went to his four sons, George (Jeremy's great-great grandfather), William, John and Caleb. It was the youngest of the brothers who would seem to have been the really proficient businessman: Caleb opened a London factory for Kilner Brothers, as they were now called. From that base, the company was able to export to all four corners of the globe.

For a time, the company prospered. It was the only British glass-bottle maker to win a medal in the 1862 Great International Exhibition in London and, over the next two decades, it won similar awards all over the world. However, at the beginning of the twentieth century, competition from abroad meant that Kilner Brothers, and quite a number of other companies, faced severe problems, and so the all-important Kilner patents were sold to a firm called United Glass Bottle.

But that was not the end of it and, intriguingly, it emerged that Jeremy's love of cars might have been echoed in his family many decades before. After selling the patents, Caleb Kilner was still a very rich man, and died leaving a huge amount of money to his son George and his son-in-law Harry Smethurst, who was married to Clarkson's great-grandmother Annie. Harry was an architect and he and his wife liked to live well, to which end it is believed that they bought a car sometime around 1901. This would have made him one of the very first people in the area to have owned such a thing.

But they were spending their money fast, which is where a good deal of it seemed to vanish, on top of which they also disinherited Clarkson's grandmother Gwendoline in the wake of a family row about what to do with the money from the sale of the patents. And so it was that Jeremy was not born into great wealth. All told, it made for a very good story.

The series was an enormous success, so much so that it was commissioned for a second run, in the course of which, that old bruiser Jeremy Paxman famously wept when confronted with the early death of a poverty-stricken relative. The other Jeremy felt no such emotion when confronted with his past. 'Hand on heart, it's not been a life-changing experience,' he said. 'Like aristocrats, or the Royal family, we all have family histories that are that old. I still don't feel any affinity for those people way back when, which I'd have enjoyed even if it was about another family.'

There was, however, a particular resonance that appeared to amuse him intently. Harry was not the only ancestor with whom Clarkson had something in common: his forebears appeared not to be too concerned about the environment, as well as owning the first cars in the area. Of course, environmental matters were not quite the hot topic they are now, but even so, it would take a very limited sense of humour not to smile inwardly at this one. 'Kilner Glass was involved in one of Britain's first ever environmental law suits, in 1871,' Clarkson revealed. 'It was brought by Lord Scarborough's estate, alleging that the smoke pouring out of Kilner's factory was killing his trees. Then there was a massive strike at the factory, with labour shipped in and police shipped up from London. It was like something from the 1980s.' A row about the environment followed by the workforce making trouble? It was hard not to sense a real note of regret that he hadn't been there.

The new, serious Clarkson was now in full swing. Another of his interests was, of course, aviation and, in the wake of the Concorde crash and its subsequent decommission – Clarkson was on its last ever flight – he became really quite thoughtful about the nature of machines. In April 2004, he appeared on *Parkinson* and mentioned the Concorde crash: when people heard about it, he said, they felt sadness for the machine itself, as well as for the terrible loss of human life. These musings prompted him to write a book on the subject – *I Know You Got Soul* – talking about the fact that machines themselves had exactly that: a kind of soul.

And he was becoming wealthier as well. The Isle of Man had always played a part in the family's life, not least since that is where Francie comes from, and so Clarkson bought a holiday home there. He managed to turn it into a political statement, noting that it is 'a thorn in the side of Tony Blair's nanny state', because there is no upper speed limit on the island. It also has tax advantages for residents, which could prove a very shrewd move in the years ahead. For now, though, Clarkson and his wife and offspring were based mainly in the Cotswolds mansion. The children were growing up, the family was moving on, and a great deal still lay ahead.

CHAPTER 12

'AWARDS NIGHTS ARE JUST A LOAD OF BLONDE GIRLS WITH THEIR BOOB JOBS OUT'

By the summer of 2005, Jeremy's ability to cause trouble had been refined into a fine art but, at the same time, his popularity had never been greater. For the point about love 'em or hate 'em types, and Clarkson most certainly is one of those, is that a lot of people do actually love them. A great many of those who do are men, of course, who would never dream of using that terminology about their hero, but, for all his many (and loudly admitted to) faults, Jeremy is a breath of fresh air; someone who dares to take a stand on issues of the day.

Clarkson also says what a great many people would like to say, but don't dare, for fear of falling foul of the politically correct brigade. He gives voice to the man on the street's secret concerns, whether it be irritating the environmental lobby – something he manages to do with such ease that it is a wonder any of them still rise to the bait – or being

187

rude about the French. And the Germans. And pretty much everyone else …

But that is the secret of his success: a blunt-talking Yorkshireman who will give it to you straight. People trust Jeremy far more than they do most celebrities for the simple reason that he tells it like it is. It is part of what made him so successful as a commentator on the motor industry: the fact that he will tell the truth, no matter how lurid the phraseology he uses, with a great deal of wit thrown in as well. He is the antithesis of every celebrity who has ever jumped on a bandwagon just for the sake of it. Even in the world of show business, he has genuinely remained his own man.

But it is in his ability to cause mischief that Clarkson really livens up the proceedings, much to the delight of all who watch. One memorable day that summer, he decided to stage an 'anti-environment' stunt at Hammersmith bus depot: he handcuffed himself to a bus. If he wanted to draw attention to himself, he most certainly succeeded in this aim – the police were called and an enraged organisation called Transport for London complained to the Broadcasting Standards Council, blaming him for causing 'a considerable amount of disruption'.

Not to be outdone, the Film Office joined in the fray, complaining that he was bringing the entertainment industry into disrepute, something many observers might feel the entertainment industry could do all by itself, without any help from Clarkson. 'Clowns like him put other people's jobs at risk,' it snapped. 'This episode makes London authorities more reluctant to co-operate with filming projects.'

With that it shot off an official complaint to the BBC, while much outrage ensued from all the usual suspects. Clarkson's response was magnificent: when one newspaper rang for a comment, Francie informed them that her husband was busy and didn't feel like talking about work at the weekend. He had, quite effortlessly, caused the maximum amount of fuss with an extremely minimal amount of effort.

If no one took heed of such stunts and the very interest groups concerned didn't allow themselves to express outrage, then the chances are that Jeremy would stop his japes. But he provides a great deal of entertainment, both for himself and everyone else, by proving over and over again quite how self-important and humourless some organisations can be. Indeed, in some ways, he is actually like the court jester of old: endlessly pricking the pomposity of the great and the good, and showing them up to look foolish with it.

And that was only one of the myriad ways he sent the hackles of the more sensitive of his observers shooting up towards the ceiling. In the aftermath of the bombings on the London transport system on 7 July 2005, when it was reported that many more people were using bicycles on the London streets, Jeremy decided that he, too, would contribute his little bit: 'Handy hints to those setting out on a bike for the first time,' he wrote. 'Do not cruise through red lights, because if I'm coming the other way, I will run you down, for fun. Do not pull up at junctions in front of a line of traffic, because if I'm behind you, I will set off at normal speed and you will be crushed under my wheels.' It does not need a particularly vivid imagination to envisage the cyclists' reaction.

Some people were pretty annoyed, not least Roger Geffen, campaigns manager of the CTC, the national cyclists' organisation. 'We were unhappy that he effectively advocated running down cyclists,' he said. But Roger, at least, unlike so many others that Jeremy has managed to upset down the years, is well aware that much of what Clarkson says is calculated to annoy. 'You might say, "He's got his tongue in his cheek so why worry?"' he said. 'And fair enough, most people won't take him seriously. The trouble is that some will.'

Clarkson himself totally denies this. 'When people say that to me, I ask, "Would you do something just because I did it?" And they always say no. And I say, "Well, if you wouldn't, why do you think someone else would?"'

Indeed, most don't and that is how he manages to get away with so much. Nor should his wit be underestimated in all this. If Jeremy simply went around making boorish remarks about all and sundry, his appeal would have faded years ago, but he always manages to keep humour to the fore. Had his critics but realised it, almost everything about Jeremy is to do with the humorous impact he creates, quite as much as the sensations he so often manages to cause. If you doubt that, consider the above remark: there is no way anyone would seriously believe that Jeremy would try to run a cyclist down. It is simply that he enunciates such outrageous views.

On another occasion, he raised eyebrows by announcing that he'd taught all his children to drive in the grounds of the family home, something that might have been considered admirable were it not for the fact that two of them were still under the age of ten. But then again, why not? As long as they were on private land, with a father who is one of the most expert drivers in the country in charge, Jeremy's actions were entirely responsible – it was simply due to his public persona that he was causing such an intake of breath.

Indeed, he was being eminently reasonable. 'They're all great drivers,' he said. 'Emily's even driven a Porsche; it's sensible. When they pass their driving tests, they won't feel the need to go a zillion miles an hour and have all this aggression inside them like all the other teenage monsters on the road.' There, if you looked behind the public image, spoke a man with whom many agreed – not least because he highlighted the menace of teenage drivers.

But, of course, worrying about reckless teenage drivers was not entirely in accordance with Jeremy's blokeish image, and so, moments later, it was business as usual. Take his attitude towards people who tried to maintain safety on the roads. 'On *Top Gear*, we refer to the Health and Safety people as the PPD,' he announced. 'The programme prevention department.' *Top Gear* officials hastily assured everyone that the programme was 'pure entertainment', as indeed were the words of its most famous presenter.

As ever, people were all too willing to rise to the bait. 'I am sorry Jeremy Clarkson believed that health and safety was the "cancer of a civilised society",' said Timothy Walker, director-general of the Health and Safety Executive, in a very restrained reposte. 'I do not think the families of over 200 people killed at work each year would share his view.' Of course they wouldn't, but Jeremy was not aiming his words at them. As usual, he was taking on the received status quo, teasing those in authority like the bumptious little schoolboy he once was, and taunting the responsible people, the adults, if you like, to take him on.

And Clarkson was well aware that whatever he said was likely to cause trouble. 'He does know,' a friend once remarked. 'He doesn't care; he doesn't care what other people think. He is, despite the showbiz connections and the career, an absolutely classic Yorkshireman, like Geoff Boycott or Freddie Trueman. You can take him or leave him and he is not even interested in what your decision might be.'

And that, of course, was what made him so good at his job. 'If he'll make the politically incorrect joke about women or other nations without turning a hair, then we can be fairly sure that motoring industry PRs aren't going to get any special treatment,' said one insider.

Even the mightiest can be laid low, however, and Jeremy was now forced to enter a period of rest. Having discovered osteoarthritis in both hips some months previously, he then suffered two slipped discs in his back. Cheerily assuring his public that he was on steroids and intending to drink for Britain, Jeremy did not let the problem cramp his style. He did, however, have to be chauffeured about by Francie, an irony not lost on those who had observed the views he had sometimes aired about female drivers in the past.

As for Francie – 'It's wear and tear, brought on by years of driving fast cars and flying upside down in aeroplanes,' she said. There was some amusement from onlookers, however, when the couple were pictured with Jeremy looming over his much shorter wife, who was staggering under a load of luggage. 'Jeremy strained his back recently and was told by a doctor not to lift anything,' a *Top Gear* spokesperson said.

With rather good timing, Francie decided that what was good for the gander was good for the goose, at least when it came to cars. And so, amid much fanfare, she wrote publicly about a pursuit she'd been taking part in for nearly a decade now: endurance rallying. Indeed, Francie remarked that it was not really to Jeremy's taste, given how much he relished his creature comforts, but eight years previously she had taken part in the first Guild of Motor Endurance rally from Liège to Agadir and back. This year it was to be Reims to Monte Carlo in a Caterham CSR.

Then again, no one should have been surprised. The Clarksons were clearly a happy couple at the time, and so it was not unlikely that they should share their interests. On top of that, Francie was Jeremy's manager, and so would have had to become interested in cars, whether she had been naturally so inclined or not. In the event she didn't win, but she did approve of the car, offering the verdict, 'Get one and show your husband you can put your foot down.'

Jeremy, meanwhile, continued to recover from his years of wear and tear. His critics, however, were in no way mollified by this spate of personal suffering and let him know it in no uncertain way, in fact, in a manner that made headlines across the country. And for once, it was not Clarkson who managed to create the dust-up, but one of the numerous individuals he had managed to offend with his points of view. And, if truth be told, someone should have seen this coming.

Very controversially, Jeremy was due to receive an honorary degree at Oxford Brookes University for supporting high standards in engineering, mainly on the back of the Brunel programme and his wistful farewell to Concorde. He knew he was a controversial choice and started off his speech with the words, 'I fully expected to be speaking to you today covered in flour and eggs, like a giant human pancake.'

Unfortunately, he spoke too soon. A particular welcoming committee lay in wait. Students and academics alike were already unhappy that such a boisterous and non-PC figure was to be honoured, but one group meant business. It comprised a group of environmental protestors, who described Clarkson as 'a murderer – every time someone drives a car, a little bit of the earth dies'. In the event, their subsequent gesture certainly made waves: dressed in an academic gown to receive the honourary degree, he was hit in the face by a bystander with a cream pie.

But perhaps this should have been foreseen: no less than 3,000 students at Oxford Brookes had signed a petition protesting at the degree being given out. Nor were students the only objectors, the academics present, or at least a portion of them, seemed equally irate. 'Clarkson's public statements could be interpreted to be at odds with many of the university's values,' said George Roberts, the university's director of e-learning. BMW workers were also angry about the award, and Transport 2000 commented that a serious academic institution honouring Clarkson was like Scotland Yard paying tribute to Inspector Clouseau.

Jeremy, however, did not seem too upset at the turn events had taken and even managed to come across as a good sport. 'Good shot,' he announced calmly, wiping pie off his face, before remarking that the concoction was a little too sweet. Even afterwards he remained unperturbed. 'At least they didn't dig my granny up,' he said, a reference to animal rights' campaigners who desecrated the grave of a woman in Staffordshire whose family reared guinea pigs for research. He was soon back on form, though, calling his assailant an 'angry bird' and 'premenstrual'.

Of course, if you dish it out, you have to be able to take it and Jeremy was proving himself eminently capable of that. No one has come in for the sharp side of his tongue as much as environmentalists – 'My wife bought me a patio heater for our anniversary and I've always been a bit nervous of it,' he once remarked. 'Now I know the environment lot hate them so much, I'll burn them twenty-four hours a day.' With remarks like that, it was hardly surprising that one of them might finally have a sense of humour failure and suddenly get nasty with a piece of pie. Indeed, in many ways, it's a wonder this doesn't happen more often. Clarkson has upset so many people that there are only too many people ready, willing and able to take aim.

Then there's everyone else who's come in for a bit of stick. To think of a category of people is to lay into it, as far as Jeremy is concerned, and that includes just about anything. He is not afraid of retribution and he likes to cause a fuss. 'The problem with France is that, like Wales, it is a very pretty country spoiled only by the people who live there,' he once remarked, and when that was followed up by a Welshman asking why he hated Wales, he replied: 'What with the Germans and Koreans to think about, I honestly haven't time to be hating the Welsh … it's Surrey I hate … if Kent is the garden of England, then Surrey is surely the patio. It's shit.'

Again, what so many people who get upset by him tend to forget is that Clarkson is doing this deliberately. He is a professional controversialist: people switch on the television or read his columns in newspapers to see him being outrageous; they do not want him to make placatory remarks. And so Clarkson, good Yorkshireman that he is, lays it on the line, insulting one nationality here, a specific individual there, and then sits back and watches the subsequent uproar.

And it is simply so easy to provoke the environmentalists. 'Of course, there is no doubt that the world is warming up, but let's just stop and think for a moment what the consequences might be,' he pronounced. 'Switzerland loses its skiing resorts? The beach in Miami is washed away? North Carolina gets knocked over by a hurricane? Anything bothering you yet? It isn't even worthy of a shrug.'

And when he is forced to take it on the chin, or, as in the pie incident, full in the face, he does so without complaining. He would be no fun if he whinged about the extremely negative reaction he provokes in some quarters, but he doesn't. He simply gets on with it and moves on to cause mayhem once more.

His appeal is very broad, something witnessed by the fact that the two newspapers he has written for since the mid-90s, *The Sun* and *The Sunday Times*, are aimed at the opposite ends of the market. His appeal is classless, and his blokey image one that many men – and women – respond to, regardless of their own background. Indeed, people are often surprised to find that Jeremy is himself the product of a private school education – he now has a kind of classlessness that can go down equally well and equally badly on all sides.

But there's no question about it: he really does cause upset and the reaction to 'Piegate' showed quite how deeply antipathy towards him existed in some quarters. The media were not exactly devastated by the turn of events, and some went on to congratulate the pie thrower, Rebecca Lush. 'Afterwards, I had an extraordinary response with messages of support, including from several people in the media,' she said. 'I met someone who works at News International [which owns *The Sun* and *The Sunday Times*, Clarkson's two papers] who just wouldn't let go of my hand, and kept on going, "Thank you for doing that! Thank you!"'

Indeed, she had been rather enthusiastic about the whole episode, recounting breathlessly how she had stalked her prey. Clarkson had gone into a marquee, she said, continuing, 'But then he came out again, so I ran after him.' It took quite a leap for the pie to hit its target, given Clarkson's height, but still she managed it. 'He's a bloody huge guy,' she went on. 'Hitting him in the face was like playing basketball. I had to run very fast from a security guard. I don't know what you can be charged with, legally, for putting a pie on someone – and I had no idea what Clarkson might do.'

It didn't bother Jeremy one jot and, shortly after this, he

was seen mingling with the great and good at Lady Thatcher's eightieth-birthday celebrations at a lavish party at the Mandarin Oriental Hotel in London's Hyde Park. No pies were forthcoming that time.

Nevertheless, he did reflect on it shortly afterwards, when he made his views public about the event. 'It's unfortunate that I was terribly jet lagged,' he remarked. 'Otherwise I would have guessed that something was up when the photographers said, "Would you mind stepping over here, because the light is better?" They knew what was going on. And I have to say that, at the PR level, it was a fantastic result to the environmentalists. One-nil to them.'

Was it one-nil to the Greens? It was hard to say. Clarkson's reaction, both in his sangfroid and his making light of the incident lost him no fans. Nor was it he who that appeared determined not to listen to both sides. 'I don't want to be their bête noir,' he said of the Green Movement. 'I want to be the champion of ordinary people – who seem to be lectured to all the time. Look, there are two sides to the argument. I do listen, constantly, to their side of the argument. And every time they're presented with my side, they shove a pie in my face.

'I went on Jeremy Vine's radio show to discuss some aspect of the environment and they had the environmentalist George Monbiot on, and he said, on air, that if I liked 4x4s, it must be because my penis is small! He sent me a letter afterwards apologising for getting carried away, but that's the level of debate. They get together to discuss things, these people, eating their nuclear-free peace nibbles, and they're just never exposed to the other side of the argument. They say, "We live in Hackney and we think such and such a thing is wrong." And that's it. There's no doubt that we will all have to subscribe to their views eventually. In fact, to judge by the pie incident, the time has already passed.'

Indeed, Monbiot's language certainly didn't help his cause: 'I suggest that instead of getting into an overpowered 4x4 and ripping up the countryside, he responds to one of those e-mails that offers to enhance the size of his manhood,' he said.

It later emerged that Rebecca, the pie-thrower, unsurprisingly, was an activist with the organisation Roadblock, an outfit particularly appalled by Jeremy's somewhat laissez-faire attitude to environmental concerns. 'Clarkson used to be a climate-change denier,' she said, when she explained how she was finally driven to throw that pie. 'Now that position is not tenable, so he just says, "Who cares?" It's obnoxious: a selfish and irresponsible attitude and it's dressed up as laddish humour.'

Other environmental protestors queued up to agree. 'Clarkson is a class-A muppet and absolute plonker,' said Ben Stewart of Greenpeace. 'One can only assume that his jeans are restricting his blood-flow. He says things about global warming that are wrong. Also he's said that he has wet dreams about Greenpeace ships turning over. He's best ignored, but that's pretty bad.' The trouble is, though, that everyone he turned on had a difficult time ignoring him. They always wanted to be able to answer back. And Stewart, like Roger Geffen (although the former sounded even more irritated than the latter), was aware that people did listen to what Jeremy had to say.

As more emerged about Rebecca, it turned out she was as committedly pro-environment as she perceived Clarkson to be anti. She had spent four months in jail in 1993 for her role in protests against a road-building programme on Twyford Down. 'It wasn't nice, but the support we got was incredible,' she said. 'It was the first time environmental activists had been sent to prison, and it really inspired people. I received 100 letters a day. I love the countryside and I love nature, but I don't see global warming as a countryside thing – it's about the survival of our species; it's about people. And transport is the fastest-growing contributor to climate change.'

Then there were various other protests in which she managed to attract a huge amount of attention: she once chained herself to a digger and, on another occasion, managed to disrupt a meeting about the Thames Gateway bridge by snatching the microphone and running around with it and crying, 'This is a scandal. The bridge is being railroaded through. You are not listening.' Was this not, along with pie-flinging, a little bit childish, she was asked.

'You grab attention through direct action,' retorted Rebecca, and she was certainly correct about that aspect of it. 'I don't think people would have thought about these issues otherwise. Direct action is about making people think, "Why is that woman doing that?" People thought we were weird, in 1992, to risk our lives by standing in front of bulldozers. But environmentalists are always putting out messages that we're derided for until, ten to fifteen years later, the ideas have become mainstream.'

Nor was Clarkson to be her last target: the fuel protestors

were next. 'They are ignorant of basic economics,' she said. 'The government has bent over backwards for them since 2000 by not increasing fuel duty at all. They're in the Dark Ages. They have to face the reality that fuel prices are going up. That's not a radical statement, it's what the AA and the RAC are saying.'

Perhaps, given that his passion and his career are cars, it is inevitable that the environmental lobby causes him particular ire. Clarkson never misses a chance to put the boot in, and always seems totally unconcerned when he's attacked in return. He will also make wildly sweeping statements when he is on a roll, proclamations that have a lot more to do with irritating the green brigade than actually making a great deal of sense. 'Engineering is more important than environmentalism, he once declared, adding, 'Environmentalism has given the world nothing. I do have a disregard for the environment; I think the world can look after itself and we should enjoy it as best we can.'

Jeremy was perfectly happy to lay into the industry that had made him such a success as well. In the run-up to the National Television Awards, in which he was up for best TV expert against Simon Cowell, Sharon Osbourne and the increasingly famous chefs Jamie Oliver and Gordon Ramsay, Clarkson made it quite clear what he thought of the event. 'Last year I timed it to perfection,' he said. 'I was out for dinner, had my starter, ran into the Royal Albert Hall and gurned for the cameras as *Top Gear* lost, then went back to the restaurant, where my cigarette hadn't even gone out.'

And *Top Gear* was, indeed, being nominated again, as Most Popular Factual Programme, with the other contenders being

Jamie's School Dinners, *Crimewatch UK*, *Supernanny* and *Wife Swap*. Did Jeremy care? Not according to him. 'I hate awards events,' he said. 'I've been nominated for ten years and lost every single year. I'm always a bridesmaid and never a bride. Men never pick up the phone to vote, they've got better things to do. It's always the grannies and teenagers who vote. The room is full of 20,000 blonde starlets and I have no idea who they are. It's just a sea of gormless people. I really only watch *24* and *Bodies*. Awards nights are just a load of blonde girls with their boob jobs out on display.'

It is not hard to see why it was not his kind of scene. The television community is not renowned for being filled with people who choose substance over style: a lot of air kissing combined with the kind of bitchiness and back stabbing so often associated with these gatherings clearly held no appeal. Jeremy was one of the most famous of their number, but he did not actually spend that much time at high-profile showbiz parties and award shows, and so it was no surprise he wanted to avoid them this time.

Indeed, so resolute was he about his contempt for awards ceremonies that he cheerily asserted that his children actually wanted Simon Cowell to win. 'My kids watch *The Simpsons* and only pause it to turn on *X Factor*,' he said. 'They love Simon. I guarantee if you asked, "Do you want Daddy or Simon to win?" they'd pick Simon. Gordon's a great bloke as well. The trouble with all of us is we all like to wear the trousers, as it were. Sharon looks like great fun, though – she could probably keep us all in our place.'

Not that he was actually going to be there. Rather than wasting his time at an awards ceremony he didn't actually care about, Jeremy was taking part in a contest with Richard Hammond and James May. The challenge? To show that he could drive from Turin in Italy back to London faster than they could fly. The mode of transport was to be a £600,000 Bugatti. 'We're going to have a race to see who can get to Gordon Ramsay's restaurant in Chelsea first,' Clarkson cheerily announced. 'Hammond will be heartbroken he won't be at the awards; he loves preening. He'll be gutted that he'll be stuck in Italy.' It was a typically laddish and Clarksonesque way to behave.

But Clarkson was not going to stop there. Always on the lookout for new challenges, and constantly searching for the next big thing, he was now thinking about what he would do to go that one step further than he already had. After all, he'd already driven, flown and sailed in just about everything available, and so there were no obvious vehicles crying out to be ridden. He'd traced his own family history, popularised one of Britain's greatest engineers, shown himself to have an intellect as well as a way of getting under people's skin – what was left?

A great deal, of course. But in his quest to push himself ever further, make brilliant television and even better newspaper copy, Clarkson now decided on his most dangerous adventure yet, in the company of his friend and travelling companion Adrian Gill: they would be going to the Middle East, or more specifically, Iraq.

CHAPTER 13

CLARKSON STRIKES OUT

One of Jeremy Clarkson's most intense feuds had been going on for several years. It was with Piers Morgan, erstwhile editor of the *Mirror*, and it began at the turn of the millennium. Although the cause of it varies depending on who you ask, according to Jeremy it began, 'when I refused to jump ship and write for the *Mirror*, saying I'd rather write operating manuals for car stereos.' The *Mirror* is, of course, the arch rival to *The Sun*, for which Clarkson writes a column. But professional rivalry had nothing to do with it according to Piers, who insists the feud began when the *Mirror* published pictures of Jeremy kissing Elaine Bedell, his producer.

And, he claimed, they were (initially at least) a good deal kinder to Clarkson than they might have been, ringing him for a comment when the first set of pictures appeared (there were to be two) and getting a response Morgan relished repeating in full when his autobiography came out: 'Look, Piers, I'm going to tell you something now,' said Jeremy, while practically begging Piers not to run the pictures. 'I'm not capable of having an affair. You can ask my wife. I'm not physically capable.'

In due course the pictures appeared anyway, although this time around they were played down. Frances appeared merely irritated. 'Jeremy rang and told me about the pictures,' she said. 'I immediately knew it was ridiculous. People always believe there is no smoke without fire but it's simple – they work together, they're matey. They were doing exactly what I knew they were doing – it's what mates do. The paparazzi are a nuisance. I was very angry. They take photos out of context and put a story to them, this time implying he was having an affair.'

Clarkson himself denied anything untoward point-blank, and that was that: the incident merited no further comment. Until a few years later, when Jeremy was pictured kissing Elaine again. This time the *Mirror* not only ran with the story but made a great deal of fuss about it. Clarkson was incandescent. Again he denied that there was anything to it, but this time it was personal. He was out to get Piers Morgan.

The first time the opportunity really arose for a personal confrontation came some months later. In October 2003, Jeremy and Piers were both on the final Concorde flight from New York to London in the company of esteemed travellers including Joan Collins, Sir David Frost, Lord Colin Marshall (Chairman of British Airways), Jodie Kidd, Christie Brinkley, Mary Nightingale and the ballerina Darcey Bussell. As the champagne flowed, the two of them descended into their usual shenanigans. 'We are served perfectly chilled canapés, the gastronomic pleasure only slightly marred by Jeremy Clarkson deciding to throw a glass of water over me,' wrote Piers in an account of the trip, gleefully recording that an American asked Clarkson if he was a reporter.

The spat received massive coverage on account of tying in with Concorde's last flight. One diarist jubilantly remarked that Jeremy initially asked Piers to step outside, before remembering that they were at 55,000 feet, while another commented that he took one look at Piers on boarding, started rolling up his sleeves and roared, 'Let's sort it out now.' The stewards managed to get him to sit down for take-off, after which some liquid – some had it as water, others as champagne – was thrown. 'That was for my wife!' he yelled.

As ever, it stimulated reams of newsprint, but there were some people who speculated that Clarkson had set the whole thing up in advance. 'I was speaking to Jeremy the night before,' confided one source, 'and he told me he planned to do something to get back at Morgan when he could.'

This latter account was given credence by Simon Kelner, editor of *The Independent*, who was also on the flight. The night before, Kelner and Clarkson had bumped into one another in the foyer of their hotel. 'I hope I am sitting near Piers Morgan,' snapped Jeremy. 'Then you'll have a story because I'm going to punch that little shit's lights out.'

Once on board, Piers began to snipe back, thundering, 'You may be big, Clarkson, but you'll go down like a sack of shit.' In the event, fisticuffs were deferred till another occasion. But it was hard not to suspect that both men were relishing every minute of it – they were, after all, consummate showmen who loved the limelight.

The next altercation was altogether more physical. It was in March 2004 at the British Press Awards, which took place that year at the Park Lane Hilton in London. A notoriously rowdy affair at the best of times, heavy drinking had been going on for hours before Clarkson finally laid into Morgan, punching him three times and knocking him to the floor.

As ever, everyone involved managed to get maximum mileage out of the event. 'They were three pitiful blows. I have had bigger drubbings from my three-year-old son,' said Piers, who admitted he had been goading Jeremy beforehand. 'There has been a simmering volcanic rage since we published the photos of Clarkson. I upset him at the Press Awards when I suggested his wife would be happier if he did not embrace other women.'

Piers himself, however, had no intention of letting the hostilities be forgotten. As 2005's British Press Awards approached, he made reference to the last event: 'If you see Jeremy Clarkson, and he is sweating, has wonky eyes, and keeps abusing everyone who goes up on stage then be very careful,' he wrote in the form of tips on how to survive the awards ceremony. 'I made the fatal error last year of seeing him in this state and then jokily inviting him to punch me on the head, which is precisely what he then did a few hours later. Three times, quite hard, right smack on the bonce. I still have a neat two-inch scar from his ring down the right side of my forehead. Never could stand jewellery on a man.'

In the event, Jeremy actually had the last laugh, winning the award for Motoring Writer of the Year. According to the judges, 'He's streets ahead' and 'He always seems to have another gear.' Clarkson replied in suitably measured tones, with only the odd barb thrown at Morgan.

Years later, however, Piers – who by then had left his post as editor of the *Mirror* under difficult circumstances – would actually offer sympathy to Jeremy when he was forced to leave *Top Gear*. They would never be bosom buddies but the feud had simmered down by then.

★ ★ ★

Clarkson's next outing with Adrian was not for the fainthearted: a 2005 trip to Iraq to write about it for *The Sunday Times*. 'Yes, I know I could get killed,' said Jeremy solemnly. 'I'm not even taking out a film crew, as I could never ask them to do something as dangerous as this. I'm going to find a crew out there and we're going to try to film some scenes around Iraq for the show.'

As for the contents of his kitbag, Jeremy was his usual forthright self – although he couldn't resist playing it up for all it was worth: 'Bog roll, malaria tablets, diarrhoea tablets and, oh yes, a bit of body armour.' His natural showmanship made itself felt even here.

He conceded, however, that the mission was slightly beyond what he usually put his family through: Emily was now eleven, Finlo nine and Katya seven. 'My wife is being very brave,' said

Jeremy, 'my youngest ones are too little to realise what's going on but my oldest daughter has been pretty upset and there have been some tears.'

The journey had taken some planning: departure from Britain and landing in Baghdad both had to take place in the dark, to evade Islamic militants attempting to bring down the plane in either country. British militants could alert their Iraqi counterparts as to when the plane had taken off and where it was likely to land

The number of planes available for the journey was extremely limited – three in fact, according to Clarkson, and all were in a state of disrepair, forcing the trip to be postponed several times. At last, however, the duo got to Kuwait on British Airways, before making the last part of the journey by Hercules helicopter.

The trip, which was criticised in some quarters for taking great risks at a time when the situation in Iraq was highly unstable, was not without incident. Flying from Basra to Baghdad in a Hercules transporter, he came under attack three times from rocket-propelled grenades, leaving him shaken but not stirred.

'It was mostly while I was in the air, which was truly heart-stopping,' he commented. After that, insurgents launched a mortar attack on the compound where he was staying. This, of course, made the news in Britain: Clarkson had been fired at four times and escaped unscathed.

But the object of the visit was successful. A long *Sunday Times* piece sympathetically detailed the hellhole that American and

British troops found themselves in. There was also a good deal of laddish larking about, with Jeremy and Adrian staging a tank race, and Jeremy managing to film a segment for *Top Gear* from the back of an armoured Land Rover. 'I wasn't at the wheel, but I directed the piece,' Clarkson said. 'It might be a bit shaky – that will be the nerves. Hopefully we will use it on the show.'

One salient point that people who objected to the trip missed was that it provided a great deal of light relief for troops stationed in Iraq. None of Jeremy's exploits, especially racing the tanks, would have been possible without a great deal of help from the British Army, who apparently held him in very high regard.

It wasn't just the Iraqis who were out to get Clarkson though: he was also on the receiving end of some aggro closer to home. His new £1.25 million holiday home on the Isle of Man, Lighthouse Cottages, provided access to a coastal path at Langness, an area with spectacular views of the Irish Sea. Jeremy promptly upset local ramblers by calling them 'unpleasant and deeply militant dog walkers' and barring them from using the paths near his house. 'You have these clots who think they have a God-given right to trample on somebody else's garden and kill the sheep,' he added, as he put up barbed wire to keep ramblers off his land and put up signs reading, 'Langness Wildlife Trail', which guided them to a different route.

This caused uproar, with many of locals saying that they could no longer appreciate the view or watch dolphins and seals in the water. They formed an action group, pledging to fight Jeremy 'all the way'. Dick Hodge, a member of the protest committee, was incandescent: 'The Manx people have always enjoyed the right to enjoy their beautiful island,' he fumed. 'We cannot allow anyone, including Mr Clarkson, to change that.'

Jeremy's stunts continued to cause upset too. Driving around Scotland in a Land Rover Discovery, his route took him over rare plant life at the top of Ben Tongue mountain. There was concern about damage to a peat bog, with the usual furious condemnation following on hard. The first angry reaction came from John Mackenzie, Earl of Cromartie, who was the president of the Mountaineering Council of Scotland. He had offered the BBC team part of his land for Clarkson to drive on, but the programme makers didn't think it wild enough and pressed on with the alternative route instead.

The Earl was not impressed. 'The most worrying aspect of this is that it could set a precedent,' he said. 'People may well view Scotland as being a fantastic country for four by fours. The new access bill is quite distinctively for pedestrian and non-motorised access but it could be construed otherwise by less-disciplined individuals. I advised them to use an ecologically friendly site but that seems to have been ignored.'

But the BBC was adamant that there was no problem. 'We took proper precautions, it was filmed under a controlled environment and permission was sought,' said a spokesperson. 'It is in no way telling people to go off and tear up the countryside.'

Land Rover also confirmed that the BBC had obtained permission for the drive beforehand. 'I think as a utilitarian brand we are keener on use where necessary rather than just leisure use,' said a spokesman. 'But people have the right to do what they wish in this country.'

Clarkson himself remained unmoved, but still his detractors lined up. The latest to have a go were Liberal Democrat MPs Norman Baker and Tom Brake, who felt moved to table a motion calling for Clarkson to be summoned to the House of Commons to explain 'a curious and misguided attitude to the real and major threat posed by climate change'.

Jeremy's response was more in sorrow than in anger. 'Environmentalists, it seems, can't argue like normal people,' he wrote rather wearily. 'You may remember, for instance, back in the summer that a vegetarian girl, who I'd never met before, leapt from some bushes and plunged a huge banoffee pie right into the middle of my face. Then a Liberal Democrat MP called Tom Brake, who has the silliest teeth in politics, said he was going to table an early-day motion and drag me to London to watch him doing it. Now look. I don't want to see anyone's early-day motion, least of all a Liberal Democrat's, which would be full of leaf mulch. And I especially don't want to see it on a table. Why can't these people write me a letter saying, "I don't agree with you"? Why do they have to pie me and make me stand around watching a Liberal with mad teeth doing his number twos? It's beyond comprehension.'

Then, in December 2005, Clarkson almost – almost – went too far. He was testing an Oxford-built Mini and, noting that it was now owned by BMW, he allowed his fancy to have free reign. After hearing that the Mini was designed with built-in

teaspoons and teabags to give it a British touch, he referred
to it as a 'quintessentially German car': it would have, he said,
indicators that worked like a Hitler salute, 'a satellite navigation
system that only goes to Poland', and, adding in a mock
German accent, 'a fan belt that lasted for 1,000 years', as Hitler
had claimed his Third Reich would. He finished this off with
the Nazi salute.

An awful lot of people were immensely amused, but many
others were not. Even the German government was upset,
although it refrained from making a public complaint; instead,
it contacted the BBC privately, pointing out that Clarkson
could get up to six months in jail if he made the Nazi salute
on German television. Meanwhile, the German industrialist
Lanbert Courth, head of the Bayer Corporation in the UK,
called the segment 'unpleasant and disturbing'.

The BBC responded by saying 'we will investigate any
complaints in the normal way.' Clarkson responded by saying,
'My admiration for Germany as an engineering powerhouse
knows no bounds but I bet Prince Charles gets more laughs
talking to his plants. The other day I spoke to a German car
designer for four hours and he failed to make even half an
attempt at a joke in all that time. A Brit can't go four minutes
without trying to make someone laugh.'

At the beginning of 2006, it was announced that Jeremy was
to become one of a series of guest presenters on *Never Mind The
Buzzcocks*, as regular presenter Mark Lamarr had stood down:
Clarkson, like Lamarr, was cutting and very, very sharp. He also
continued to guest-host *Have I Got News For You* and helped

Gordon Ramsey cook lobster on the latter's television show. His popularity remained undimmed.

* * *

Jeremy Clarkson has suffered his fair share of life's sadness – most notably when his father died in 1994. Jeremy and his mother used that familiar Clarkson tactic of retreating behind humour to deflect pain. Shirley once said that when her husband was dying, she and Jeremy would play games such as, 'List all the illnesses dad has had this month' or 'Name all the drugs that dad's taking beginning with the letter P'.

'It's just what we do,' she said. 'It's more constructive than getting depressed.' It was certainly a coping mechanism, although Clarkson has said publicly that the death of his father affected him very deeply. But that was a side of him the public very rarely saw.

Then, in September 2006, Jeremy Clarkson and James May – along with the rest of the nation – were horrified when their co-presenter Richard Hammond was nearly killed in a crash. Hammond had been attempting to break the land speed record of 300mph in a Vampire dragster when it overturned, leading to severe criticism of the BBC's health and safety policy – especially when it emerged that he'd had only a few hours training in the car beforehand.

Richard was lucky to escape the crash alive. Yorkshire Air Ambulance was summoned to the scene and airlifted him to Leeds Infirmary. Richard, clearly unaware of what was happening to him, was insistent that he should continue doing his job.

'We managed to keep him talking until we reached hospital,' said Darren Axe, one of the air ambulance paramedics. 'There were no obvious injuries but it was clear that he'd suffered severe head trauma. The flight took only twelve minutes. But it seemed a lot longer to me. I kept asking the pilot, "Are we there yet?"'

Everyone went into a state of shock. Although Hammond was later to stage a full recovery, initially there were real fears that he might either die or suffer permanent brain damage.

Richard's wife, Mindy, rushed to be at his side. 'I know he'll get through this,' she said. 'He's the strongest man in the world. He's a bit daft, but I love him to bits. We're all going to be there with him.'

It put the BBC in a very difficult situation, forcing it to issue a statement about *Top Gear* which denied condoning 'irresponsible or dangerous activities'. The Health and Safety Executive announced it would be launching an investigation as this was, to all effects, a workplace accident, while motor experts said an amateur like Hammond should never have been involved in such a dangerous stunt.

Jeremy himself said he was 'absolutely devastated.' He drove from London to Leeds, where Richard was in the hospital, and mounted an overnight vigil at his friend's bedside.

'James May and I are at the hospital in Leeds where Richard remains in intensive care,' he said. 'Obviously at this time both he and his family are the most important concerns we have.

It must be devastating for his wife Mindy and his two utterly adorable children. I would just like to say how heartened Richard will be when I tell him just how many motorists and truck drivers on my way here wound down their windows to say they were rooting for him. Both James and I are looking forward to getting our "Hamster" back.'

He couldn't resist the odd tease, however. 'I was being nice to him for a change,' he said. 'But I wasn't getting any reaction. He probably thought, "That sounds like Clarkson but it can't be – he's saying nice things." He was lying peacefully with a black eye but didn't react so I tried something else. I said: "The reason you're here is because you're a crap driver." He then smiled at me. It was an amazing moment, very moving.'

In actual fact, the speed of Hammond's recovery amazed everyone. Within two days he was managing to talk and to take a few steps, something Jeremy himself was only too happy to report. 'In the wee small hours Richard Hammond suddenly sat up in bed, opened his eyes and asked what had happened,' he said. '"You've been in a car accident," I said. "Was I driving like a twat?" he asked before getting out of bed and walking, shakily, to the lavatory. Despite all the odds, it seemed we'd got our hamster back.'

Shortly afterwards, Richard was transferred to a private hospital in Bristol where he was to make a full recovery. Jeremy now deemed his friend well enough to admit that he, James and Richard had talked about what they'd do if one of them died in a stunt. 'We decided that after the announcement of the death in the following week's show, the next word should be "anyway",' he said. 'So if the Hamster had ever careered through the Pearly Gates in a 200mph fireball, I would put on a sombre face, say Richard Hammond had died and after a small pause, add: "Anyway, the new Jag…" It was a sort of a joke. But then this week it sort of wasn't.'

The depth of the affection Hammond was held in by the public became clear when it emerged that £140,000 had been raised to benefit Yorkshire Air Ambulance, to be put towards a second helicopter. His family had asked that, rather than send flowers, well-wishers should make a donation to the service, which they well and truly did.

As Richard continued to recover, the BBC decided to delay showing the new series until he was completely well again. 'It has to be those three,' said Top Gear's executive producer Andy Wilman (a statement that carries some resonance now). 'I wouldn't do it – couldn't do it – without Richard. We've shot most of this series but we won't do anything with it until he's better, because he's it.' Filming eventually began again in October.

There was certainly a great deal of comment that followed this, asking if it was right that amateur drivers, no matter how talented or knowledgeable, should be asked to engage in such dangerous activities. Motoring journalist Neil Lyndon was one such commentator. 'The people who should be examining their consciences and questioning their own responsibilities are the BBC producers and executives who have turned Top Gear into a stunt show of evermore dangerous capers,' he wrote in the Daily Mail.

'As any of the show's viewers will know, *Top Gear* has long been a disaster that was just waiting to happen. For its presenters are actively encouraged to burn the tyres to shreds and generally subject every car to the kind of handling it might get from a joyriding yob. The result? *Top Gear* trashes cars all the time… Put simply, an adolescent, law-breaking recklessness and indifference to the value of cars is now fundamental to *Top Gear's* idea of entertainment. How many viewers, for instance, must wonder if Jeremy Clarkson and the other presenters have acquired an international exemption from speed limits – or if all the police forces of Europe are turning a blind eye – every time we see them racing across the continent in a trio of 200mph supercars?'

Jeremy fought back. 'Today, people who have absolutely no idea at all of how television works (yes, columnist Neil Lyndon – that's you, you sanctimonious, rent-a-soundbite little turd) are saying that our producers push us to do more and more dangerous stunts in a bid for ratings,' he wrote. 'Rubbish. Our producers spend their whole lives filling in health and safety forms and asking, "Are you sure?" It's the presenters who come up with the hare-brained ideas and trans-continental races… not the backroom boys or the suits.'

Further confirmation of the popularity of *Top Gear's* presenters – and indeed of the programme itself – came with winning Most Popular Factual Programme at the National Television Awards. Jeremy collected the award. 'Richard knows that we've won and he's absolutely thrilled,' he said. 'Now he's won he thinks he is Napoleon and can conquer all of Europe.'

And then, in a lighthearted aside to his absent colleague, he added, 'I told you if one of us had a car accident we'd win this.'

After that it was back to business as usual. By this time, Clarkson's wealth was reflected in his increasingly valuable car collection: a Lamborghini Gallardo Spyder, a Mercedes-Benz SLK55, a Volvo XC90, a Ford Focus and an ex-military Land Rover Defender. He was expanding his professional range too, giving voice to the character Harv, Lightning McQueen's agent, in the British version of the hit animated film *Cars*.

Jeremy, clearly feeling that his softer side had been on show for far too long, also took on the caravanning community. He hosted the MPH '06 motor show first at the Birmingham NEC, and then at London's Earls Court, and in the course of the evening wrecked two caravans. Caravanners were, predictably, outraged. There were furious protests outside the show, as well as stickers and badges bearing the legend, 'Hate Clarkson, Love Caravans.' Clarkson himself was unmoved. 'When I come to power, caravans will be banned,' he said.

The show also contained some not-so-gentle ribbing of Richard, in the shape of a speeded-up wheelchair – but the man himself wasn't concerned. A few months after the accident, he revealed he was driving again and had taken Mindy out for a spin in his Morgan sports car. 'Now I feel more like me,' he said. 'As I got into the driving seat it felt like I was back where I belonged. It was wonderful to be away from everything, being able to tootle around the lanes in the foothills of the Malverns in Gloucestershire on a sunny Sunday afternoon.

'During the last two months there have a number of moments

I will never forget and this is one of them. I have really missed driving and the freedom that comes with it. I didn't realise how much until today. Mindy was a bit damp-eyed. She has been my driver for the last few weeks and I have been dependent on her. Now I'm looking forward to taking her out for a drive and a nice lunch this week.'

At the MPH '06 motoring show there had been another *Top Gear*-related crash, but this one was rather less serious. James May took a tumble when he rode a shopping trolley into ten giant skittles, falling out and spraining his wrist. He acknowledged that the crash – which took place at about 20mph – was not quite in Richard's league. 'It's quite pathetic, really,' said a rather embarrassed James. 'It turned out to be nothing more than a slight sprain. I can ride a bicycle, hold a pen, everything. The aspirins and plasters man had a look at it and said it was probably okay. Richard called and couldn't resist taking the piss.'

Jeremy was apparently seen falling over shortly afterwards when trying to tie his shoelaces, but no one seemed to get too het up about that. Indeed, there were much bigger things to worry about – namely, the potential ending of one of the most popular television series ever screened in Britain. Could it really be true that *Top Gear* was about to come to an end?

It did seem that the unthinkable was about to happen. Real doubt had been cast over the future of the show by none other than Clarkson himself. It seemed that something was amiss when he ended the most recent series by saying, 'We don't know when we'll be back,' and echoed this early in 2007 when the BBC announced plans for a one-off special in the summer: 'After last week's *Top Gear*, the TV announcer said it would be back in the summer. Can I just say, "It won't be,"' he contradicted.

The BBC promptly refuted this: '*Top Gear* will come back,' said a spokesman. 'A summer special is planned and *Top Gear* will return in the autumn. We're expecting all three boys to present the programmes.' Confusion reigned.

It seemed the problem was that the three presenters were unhappy with the direction the show was taking. They, understandably, wanted the cars to be at the heart of it, while the producers were keener on featuring celebrity guests.

Urgent talks must have been held behind the scenes, because it wasn't long before Jeremy was cheerfully contradicting himself. 'Everyone seems to think the programme is finished or that I've left,' he announced. 'Well, sorry to disappoint you all but it isn't and I haven't. *Top Gear* ... will be back in the autumn.' It was good news to literally millions of fans worldwide; Clarkson by now had a huge global following.

Meanwhile, it was finally confirmed that Richard's crash would be shown on television – by Jeremy himself. 'Half the world wants to see the crash so I'm sure we'll show it,' he said. 'We're looking into whether we've enough footage of a good quality ... I imagine we'll be using it in the first show. Richard has no idea what happened to him so he'll be as keen as everyone else to see it.' It was indeed shown, and Richard appeared on screen to discuss it at length.

Back in the world of Clarkson, Jeremy's appetite for a spat remained as strong as ever. His latest target was Channel 4 newscasters: all they had to do, he said, was turn up for work in a garish tie, read excerpts from *The Guardian* and go home. This prompted a furious rejoinder from Jon Snow. 'Well what do you have to do on a motoring programme?' he snapped. 'All you have to do is get in the car and push your foot down. Am I a fan of Clarkson's show? No, I'm a little fan belt, actually. I've only watched *Top Gear* on BBC World in very far-flung places where there's nothing else on telly.'

Jeremy didn't care. Nor did he appear unduly concerned when the May issue of *GQ* magazine put him at number ten on the list of Britain's worst dressed men. Given that the same magazine also labelled Pete Doherty as Britain's seventh best-dressed man, perhaps his indifference was understandable.

Next, Clarkson turned his attention to Malaysia or rather (to be fair) to the Malaysian car Perodua Kelisa. He called it 'unimaginative junk, with no soul, no flair and no passion' on *Top Gear*, before attacking it with a sledgehammer, hanging it from a crane and blowing it up. He followed that up by writing: 'This is without doubt the worst car, not just in its category but in the world. The inside is tackier than Anthea Turner's wedding and you don't want to think what would happen if it bumped into a lamppost. Also its name sounds like a disease.'

The Malaysian government was outraged. 'From 2001 to 2007, Perodua exported more than 2,400 units of Kelisa to the United Kingdom and the distributor had never received any negative response,' said minister Datuk Abdul Raman Suliman, before going on to criticise Clarkson as 'like a football commentator who does not play football'.

But while he might have retained the power to offend, he also certainly continued to amuse. In June 2007, a petition on the Downing Street website demanding 'Make Jeremy Clarkson Prime Minister' attracted more than 7,600 signatures. What would Clarkson do in his first hundred days in office? 'I'd sack everybody and then go to the pub and put my feet up.'

Towards the end of 2007, he also became a hero to many when he took on a gang of hoodies. Out with daughter Katya to celebrate her ninth birthday at the indoor ski slope in Milton Keynes, the family was surrounded by teenagers who simply wouldn't leave them alone. Utterly exasperated, Jeremy finally put his hands around the neck of one of the boys.

'I was standing there, holding this boy by the scruff of his neck – and instead of worrying about being stabbed I was actually thinking, "I'm going to get done for assault if I'm not careful,"' Clarkson said afterwards. 'I therefore put him down, and in a flurry of hand gestures involving various fingers he was gone. Plainly this boy's parents are useless, allowing him to be out on the streets, harassing passers-by at will.' Another member of the gang, a teenage girl, promptly reported the incident to the police, but in the event no charges were brought.

That petition was still on the Downing Street website at the beginning of 2008. It had garnered over 31,000 signatures. *Top Gear* was continuing to soar in popularity; the studio audience waiting list was an average 100,000 and could sometimes go as high as 300,000 – and there was only capacity in the studio for 500. Unusually for such a long-running television series, its popularity seemed to be getting greater as time went on.

Jeremy was still up to his old tricks, with he and James May both managing to upset the Scout movement when they reviewed the Skoda Scout car. 'I suppose every summer it goes off to the country and is touched inappropriately,' said James.

'No, no, James,' said Clarkson. 'That's the Skoda Catholic Church.'

Jeremy also sailed pretty close to the wind in the summer of 2009. The media climate had changed in the wake of the Russell Brand/Jonathan Ross fiasco, and so rather than picking on a vulnerable individual or group, Clarkson went for Gordon Brown. The Prime Minister was a big enough boy to stand up for himself, though Jeremy not only used bad language but made fun of his disability, too.

'I get into trouble talking about Gordon Brown, the silly cunt,' said Clarkson in the audience warm-up to an episode of *Top Gear*, adding for good measure that he was 'a one-eyed Scottish idiot'. BBC Two controller Janice Hadlow was in the audience and, according to insiders, distinctly not amused.

The BBC, perhaps reluctant to get into yet another controversy over one of its star presenters, was keen to play the whole thing down. 'There was a discussion about the programme,' said a BBC spokesperson, denying that Jeremy had been asked to apologise. 'It is certainly not an ongoing issue. Janice went to watch a recording of *Top Gear* as it is BBC Two's top-rated programme, and as controller of BBC Two, she holds both the programme and Jeremy in high regard. After the recording, she and Jeremy had a discussion about the programme as controllers and presenters often do.'

Indeed, having just publicly insulted Gordon Brown, the Tories promptly got it in the neck from Clarkson, too. They had just criticised the appointment of Lord Alan Sugar as Enterprise Tsar, saying this would make the BBC biased. This was 'strange', said Jeremy, adding, 'Not that long ago the self-same Tories asked me – a BBC man through and through – to join their team.' In actual fact, although Clarkson's values probably propelled him towards the Conservatives rather than Labour, he was not a party political animal at all. As a maverick, he would never be able to toe the party line.

That much was highlighted by the latest *Top Gear* controversy, in which he made a spoof advertisement for the German-owned Volkswagen Scirocco TDI: 'Berlin to Warsaw in one tank,' it ran. Up to 100 viewers complained, as did the Polish embassy. 'We understand that Mr Clarkson often jokes about various European nations, about Germans or the French,' said embassy spokesman Robert Szaniawski. 'But we believe that a joke about the Nazi German invasion of Poland is not a proper way to make people laugh. We think the tragedy of the situation – the outbreak of the Second World War – should not be the butt of jokes.'

Jeremy wasn't the slightest bit concerned, but it did emphasise how mixing politics and humour could be a minefield. Controversy was his métier; diplomacy was not. He was even prepared to be rude about the *Top Gear* audience, admitting that women often got pushed to the front.

'We get 500 people coming to our show each week and most of them are oafs,' he said in an address at the Edinburgh

International Television Festival. 'Who would you rather have in our shots? [But] I think a girl [presenter] would be a disaster, seeing the chemistry we have now. You bring a girl in and you start taking the piss out of her and that would look like bullying. I remember when we were doing the original screen tests and BBC people were insisting we had to have a girl after we had selected Hammond, so we just got James May.'

A BBC spokesman felt moved to comment: 'Jeremy, James and Richard look like oafs, as do most car blokes, so it's not like they are separating themselves from the audience,' he said.

One of the problems with constantly taunting everyone, however, is that sometimes people lash back. In September, as part of an environmental protest called Climate Rush, Jeremy was targeted as a climate change 'denier'. A group of seven women dressed as suffragettes turned up at the Clarkson homestead in a van fuelled by chip oil, and promptly dumped a load of horse manure on Jeremy's lawn. They carried with them a banner reading: 'This is what you're landing us in.' 'I'm dumping dung at Jeremy Clarkson's gates, so he might understand that his attitude will land us all in the shit,' said a woman named Tamsin Omond. Jeremy declined to comment.

Nor was he changing his mind about anything else. While praising Vicki Butler-Henderson, presenter of *Fifth Gear*, as one of the best drivers he knew, he remained adamant that female presenters would still be wrong for *Top Gear*. 'The problem is that television executives have got it into their heads that if one presenter on a show is a blond-haired, blue-eyed heterosexual boy, the other must be a black Muslim lesbian,' he wrote in his *Top Gear* blog. 'Chalk and cheese, they reckon, works. But here we have *Top Gear* setting new records after six years using cheese and cheese. It confuses them.'

There was certainly nothing wrong with the current line-up. They continued to amuse with their scrapes, the latest being James May coming a cropper in a hot air balloon that veered off its path while he was racing Richard Hammond in a Lamborghini. The fact that the problem was caused by the weather gave particular delight to some.

And Clarkson's almost pathological desire to offend showed no sign of receding. When *Top Gear* went to Romania to film, he donned a hat, started talking about 'Borat country' and added, 'I'm wearing this hat so the gypsies think I am one. I'm told they can be violent if they don't like the look of you.' The Romanian government complained. Next, the trio appeared on the pitch at Middlesbrough – wearing the shirts of Newcastle United, Middlesbrough's deadly rivals.

But whatever the naysayers thought, Jeremy and his cronies could do no wrong with the viewers. As the BBC became increasingly po-faced and health and safety regulations closed down anyone trying to have a little fun, they continued to thumb their noses at the rest of the world and get on with what they did best.

A *Top Gear* special was shown between Christmas and the New Year. In it, the three made their way from Bolivia's Amazon basin to the coast of Chile in three four by fours bought on the cheap. It was exciting stuff. 'There were gut-wrenchingly steep drops inches away and no barriers,' confessed Richard Hammond. 'I thought I was going to die.'

Fittingly, *Top Gear* was voted favourite TV programme of the decade. Clarkson had triumphed again.

CHAPTER 14

AROUND THE WORLD WITH CLARKSON

I t was a challenge for *Top Gear* to constantly to come up with new hi-jinks, but it was one to which the show invariably rose. At the beginning of 2010, there was speculation that the programme would be made into some kind of road movie, with our heroes driving around the world in a series of old cars; the film (which never actually materialised) was briefly known as 'Around the World in 80 Bangers'.

It was all grist to the mill, as were the various controversies rattling on in the background: climate change, reckless driving, as well as the fight to close off the land around his Isle of Man home, which Jeremy had by now lost. But he hadn't lost his talent to create controversy or to amuse.

'There is nothing quite as joyous as leaving the hustle and bustle of a superheated Third World hellhole and being greeted on the big BA jumbo by a homosexual with a cold flannel and refreshing glass of champagne,' he said in one bon mot. 'Take that away from us and we may as well all be Belgian.'

Subsequently asked (by Alastair Campbell) if he was anti-gay, Clarkson vehemently denied it, but then added that he 'demands the right not to get bummed' – a comment which drew gasps from the *Top Gear* audience (it wasn't broadcast) and condemnation from gay rights groups across the land.

There was more controversy – although, unusually, not of his own making – when Clarkson became embroiled in the row over whether ex-racing driver Ben Collins should be allowed to unveil himself as The Stig. The courts had ruled in his favour when he wanted to publish his autobiography, leading to some caustic comments by Jeremy during a charity auction.

'As you may know, we've had a problem with The Stig,' he commented. 'Everyone now knows his real name. It's The Twat. Actually to give him his full name, it's The Greedy Twat.' He was clearly hurt, complaining widely that Collins had come round to the Clarkson household for drinks while, in secret, he was writing his book.

Money had become something of a sore point at that moment. The BBC had been coming under immense pressure to reveal the salaries of their most highly paid stars and Jeremy was one of them. But it was a mark of his popularity that he didn't come in for anything like the criticism of some of his peers.

Ben Collins was also a bit miffed, not least because Jeremy had called him (and all racing drivers) 'a bit thick', before advertising for a replacement with the words 'he or she [a nice touch] must understand that no one, under any circumstances, should ever rat on their friends'.

'Calling me greedy is a bit hypocritical,' Collins retorted in an interview with the *Daily Express*. 'One reason Jeremy and his compatriots are going after me is their own financial interest... They're saying I've damaged the brand but I think that's unfair. I've served that brand very loyally for eight years and have helped to build it up. Jeremy seems to show a misunderstanding of what I've done for the show. Me leaving is not meant to be me poking them in the eye.'

The very bad blood was not helped by the trio of presenters firing gunshots at a cardboard cutout of The Stig on the show, prompting a spate of complaints. But it's also possible that Jeremy's ill humour was prompted by problems in his personal life. For it was now that his marital problems with Frances began to emerge.

It was a little known fact that Frances was actually Jeremy's second wife. He had been very briefly married once before, to Alexandra James in 1989, until she left him for one of his friends, Stephen Hall, just months into the marriage. He had met Alexandra, who was educated at a nunnery, when she was seventeen and he was twenty-two. They married at a Hampshire church seven years later, something that Jeremy rarely ever spoke about, not least because he had been very badly hurt. As he once said, 'The worst way anyone can dump you is by going off with your best friend.'

And that would have been that, were it not for the fact that Alexandra then alleged the pair actually had an affair after Jeremy got married again – which allegedly lasted, on and off, for about seven years. As she tried to go public with the claims, Clarkson promptly took out an injunction to stop her. It didn't really work. This was the age of social media and, while he might have been able to stop her going to the 'official' media at that exact moment, the news that he had taken out the injunction – and why – quickly became widespread. It was an open secret on Fleet Street and after a year, in October 2011, Jeremy dropped all pretence.

'Injunctions don't work,' he told the *Daily Mail*. 'You take out an injunction against somebody or some organisation and immediately news of that injunction and the people involved and the story behind the injunction is in a legal-free world on Twitter and the internet. It's pointless. You used to be able to take out an injunction and then just sit on it. But as a result of a recent court case you are now ultimately forced by the courts to go to trial – which is unbelievably expensive. If you win, news leaks out on the internet. If you lose, you then get raped by your opponent's legal fees.'

Now Alexandra could speak out and people could 'either believe it or not, it's up to them'. It essentially heralded the beginning of the end of Jeremy's second marriage, which was damaged too greatly to come back from all this.

Jeremy shrugged off the speculation about his private life and just got on with things, laughing off reports that almost 50,000 people had signed a new petition calling for him to be made Prime Minister. However, he swiftly prompted more complaints when he and Hammond donned burkas to play a trick on James May. They were laughed off too, as were those after Richard called Mexican cars 'lazy, feckless, flatulent and overweight'. The BBC apologised to the Mexican ambassador. While the jibe was not actually Jeremy's, he somehow attracted at least some of the blame.

There was also a row with former Labour Deputy Prime Minister John Prescott, although Prezza had gone on the show and managed to hold his own.

'What in the name of all that's holy were you thinking when you said, "Let's put a bus lane on the M4"?' asked Clarkson.

'I'm going to introduce you to a revolutionary thought,' said Prescott. 'You can go slower and you can get there quicker and that's to do with flow.' He certainly wasn't given an easy ride, receiving boos from the audience and at one point getting to his feet to remonstrate with them. 'Sit down,' Jeremy snarled.

The series was followed by the *Top Gear* Live tour. Then, in April 2011, came the first public sign that something was wrong in the Clarksons' marriage.

Jeremy was pictured with a leggy blonde called Phillipa Sage, who was working with the *Top Gear* team; the pictures suggested intimacy, but both point-blank denied an affair. Jeremy hastily took a holiday with his family in the Caribbean, but that was the start of a game of cat and mouse with the press. Phillipa would be out of sight for months and then the two would be pictured again, sometimes kissing. It became obvious pretty quickly that they were more than just good friends.

Phillipa, or Pip as she was known to friends, was to become a long-term fixture in Jeremy's life, someone he could turn to when matters got a little heated, as they were so often prone to do. Then forty-two years old, with a five-year-old son, Alfred, by ex-partner and leisure company owner Edward Taylor, Phillipa was a former beautician at a Hertfordshire country club. She'd also worked as a masseuse for footballers at Tottenham Hotspur and Queens Park Rangers. Now resident in Woolmer Green, she lived close to her parents and two brothers.

'She wasn't common like a WAG,' a friend observed. 'She was nicely spoken and attractive. She comes from a good background and her family were well-off. Away from work she liked to socialise and loved fast cars. She once had a convertible which she nicknamed Robbie the Roadster.' In other words, she had quite a lot in common with Clarkson.

Jeremy continued to laugh off the reports, telling friends that he was a 'babe magnet' while reassuring his mother that he hadn't turned into Tiger Woods. But friends were concerned, warning privately that Frances had contributed a huge amount to his career and that without her he'd be lost. Bizarrely, socialite Jemima Goldsmith (or Khan, as she then was) was dragged into the furore with rumours abounding that she too had had a fling with Jeremy – although this was a by-product of the confusion caused by the injunction, at that point still in place, and totally untrue.

It was around this time that Jeremy started spending more time in London, writing wistfully about what is essential in life after moving into an unfurnished flat. In private, at least, it was becoming increasingly apparent that the marriage was falling apart.

Nor was there a shortage of drama elsewhere. Because of

his house in the country, Jeremy found himself a part of the 'Chipping Norton set', which also included Rebekah Brooks, erstwhile *Sun* editor and chief executive of News International, and Prime Minister David Cameron. He was also at the centre of news articles about who he socialised with, said in some quarters to be the elite who ruled Britain. As ever, he laughed it off – although, as this was when the phone hacking scandal got underway in earnest, he can't have been quite so amused when it emerged that, in 1997, as his career started to take off, private investigators had been hired to see if they could dish any dirt on his public school days.

Pausing briefly to upset George Michael, Salford and Birmingham (as Richard Hammond is a Brummie), Jeremy then proceeded to cause outrage by confessing to eating what appeared to be about half the endangered species of the world. 'I absolutely love trying unusual delicacies when I am abroad. I have eaten alligators, ostrich and a thrush,' he said. 'I've also eaten the flipper from a seal, a shark cooked in urine and the still-beating heart of a snake, washed down with vodka. In this country we eat overpriced rubbish. And we have a stupid, narrow-minded approach to anything that doesn't moo, baa, oink or cluck. We should expand our horizons. We should eat more things.'

Cue People for the Ethical Treatment of Animals: 'Clarkson may be clever with cars, but he's a buffoon in other areas. When it comes to showing compassion for others, from animals to foreigners, he makes the Duke of Edinburgh's remarks about farming leopards for their pelts seem tame.'

He was also extremely good at winding people up. As was pointed out at the time, even when he wasn't actually doing anything he still managed to make the news. Nor did the man – or rather woman – in the street seem to hold any of this against him, with one poll claiming women over forty visualised their ideal man as a cross between Jeremy and Hugh Laurie.

Yet he still managed to provoke outrage wherever he went. Very many noses were put out of joint when Jeremy and James were seen parking in disabled bays whilst testing electric cars, provoking harsh words from Disabled Motoring UK and a more placatory response from the BBC. Then Nissan protested that *Top Gear* had staged an incident in which the electric car Jeremy was driving ran out of power.

He did later admit he knew the charge was low, but mounted a furious defence of the show in the wake of claims that professional drivers faked the difficult stunts. 'It's complete rubbish,' he said. 'If I say I drove a Lamborghini and got to 207mph, then that's what I did. I was in the car.'

Behind all the bonhomie, however, there were hints of a certain sadness in his personal life. Jeremy publicly bemoaned the fact that he couldn't use a washing machine, earning the reprimand of 'dimwit' from James, but the fact that he admitted he had to use one indicated a big change in his circumstances.

Although it was not yet publicly admitted, he and Frances were now mostly living apart. They continued to make the odd joint appearance, but they were increasingly rare and it was at around this time that the injunction was lifted over Jeremy's relationship with Alexandra.

That particular matter was now beyond repair, not least when Alexandra hotly denied claims that she had tried to blackmail Jeremy to the tune of £300,000 in order to stay quiet. It was an ugly twist, and there was certainly no love lost between them now. 'He was too big for his boots even back before he was famous,' said Alexandra. 'At parties he craved attention and was fat and opinionated. I had no idea how famous he'd become. He chain-smoked and was just a fat slob. But he was very smart and anyone who couldn't keep up was doomed.'

But while his private life was becoming ever more complex, he was as popular with the public as ever. The *Top Gear* satnav, the TomTom, of which 54,000 were made, was voiced by Jeremy; in the longer term, however, BBC bosses decided it breached internal guidelines which specified the show's presenters shouldn't endorse motoring products. Instructions included, 'Turn left, then go straight on until I have to shout at you again for ignoring me' and 'Keep right, then take the motorway. You can't miss it – it's a big lump of tarmac full of caravans and traffic cones.' Almost inevitably, as soon as the ban was announced the TomTom sold out. One newspaper ran a competition to win one and was inundated with entries. Everyone wanted to be shouted at by Jeremy.

There was one possible exception, though. Now free from the injunction, it seemed that no one could prevail upon Alexandra to be quiet either. She appeared in an interview on ITV with Adrian Chiles. 'Four months after I left him I realised I'd made a mistake and it's had a huge impact on my life and has affected me hugely for the rest of my life,' she said. 'Having

Jeremy Clarkson as my ex-husband has had a huge influence on my life. I had no idea how great an influence that was going to be. I had the courtesy to tell him that I wanted to write a book and his reaction was to slap a super-injunction on me. I had no intention of writing anything nasty about him; I was going to be completely lovely about him. I wasn't going to mention the affair… I was going to do my book, my life and the impact his fame has had on my life. There wasn't that much to do with him, I wanted to write my story. He's shot himself in the foot. If he hadn't wanted any mention of the affair then he shouldn't have taken the injunction out.'

Her subsequent marriage to Stephen Hall, which produced two children, had also broken down. Kate Birchenough, the new partner of the property developer, gave a revealing peep behind the scenes. 'Poor Steve got caught up in it,' she told *The Sunday Mirror*. 'He would always play second fiddle to Jeremy. It has been very painful for Steve because it was so long ago but Alex still wounded him greatly. This has been hanging over us for a very long time and the injunction being lifted is a huge relief.'

Stephen and Jeremy had 'no kind of relationship now,' she said. 'Regardless what you think of Jeremy, he does not deserve all the dirt that Alex is throwing at him and Steve knows that, too. We only ever talk to her because of the kids and we try to keep her at arm's length. This injunction has meant her name has been mentioned more often in conversations than we would like.'

It was no one's finest hour.

Jeremy was clearly keen to move on and was soon up to his old tricks: striking public sector workers should be executed in front of their families; animals should be 'cute, delicious or magnificent'; trains shouldn't stop after they've hit a person. Twitter lit up, but it shouldn't have bothered. Jeremy's job was to create controversy and he did it better than anyone – although that comment about the strikers did elicit a rare apology, after both the Prime Minister and the Leader of the Opposition got dragged into the ensuing row. ('That's obviously a silly thing to say,' said David Cameron. 'I'm sure he didn't mean it.' Boris Johnson, on the other hand, was very supportive.)

The unions were livid and over 32,000 people complained to the BBC. But Clarkson was, by this stage, untouchable. As one wag put it, what he was apologising for had generated a huge amount of publicity for his new DVD. In fact, in the wake of the row sales shot up by 50 per cent. The BBC did, however, postpone an episode of *QI* in which he featured, but for Jeremy it was clearly water off a duck's back.

Nor did it stop him. He followed up the comment on train fatalities by writing that people who commit suicide by jumping on the tracks are selfish, provoking yet another furore. This time round though, it was suggested that this wasn't just Clarkson being deliberately provocative, that his judgment may have been affected by the turmoil in his private life. With his first wife on the attack, his second finally having had enough and a girlfriend sitting quietly in the shadows, even by Jeremy's standards it was a pretty torrid time.

'There's a feeling he's more vulnerable than he should be,'

fretted one BBC insider. But despite whatever concerns they might have had, he remained both their most popular and profitable presenter. It was in the interests of no one, least of all Jeremy himself, to change that.

But Alex chimed in: 'Jeremy's the same now as he's always been,' she said. 'The problem is that now he says these things to an audience of millions rather than to a few friends. He shows no compassion, but then Jeremy doesn't think about the repercussions of his actions. He never has.'

Many would say it wasn't really a question of compassion but of an urge to provoke. But with the BBC very sensitive to public ire in the wake of the Ross/Brand/Andrew Sachs fiasco, the message was clear: do exercise caution before opening your mouth.

But Clarkson continued to rise above it all: pictured surrounded by a bevy of beauties in the middle of the *Top Gear Live* show in Australia while soaking up the sun on a powerboat with James.

The BBC was sticking up for its man as well. 'I don't intend to sack him,' said then Director General Mark Thompson, answering Labour MP Jim Sheridan's comment that Clarkson was a 'luxury you can't afford' at the House of Commons Culture, Media and Sport Committee. 'Although clearly he's a polarising figure for the BBC, there are many millions of people who enjoy and support Jeremy Clarkson. That has to be balanced against a couple of flippant remarks. Well over 20 million people watch *Top Gear* in a given season. It gets a very high rating from the public for quality. People watch that programme expecting often outspoken humour from Clarkson. I believe it is absolutely clear to anyone who watches the clips, perhaps not who reads a section of the transcript, these remarks are said entirely in jest and not to be taken seriously. In my view Jeremy Clarkson's remarks were absolutely and clearly intended as a joke. I can't see how anyone could watch that programme and see the comments as a piece of public policy.'

Of course Jeremy had been joking, but the feeling now was that he was pushing his luck. Nor did it stop Ofcom from announcing it would be investigating him – though ultimately he'd be cleared.

Clarkson was still able to laugh all the way to the bank, earning over £2 million in 2011 alone under the terms of a lucrative deal struck with the BBC. Apart from the £350,000 performance fee he earned from the corporation, he also had a stake in a company called Bedder 6, set up on the back of the show's success, and even that didn't take into account all his external earnings. Jeremy Clarkson had become an extremely wealthy man.

India became the latest country to receive the Clarkson treatment when a road trip filmed during the summer was broadcast. Everyone had been assured they would be highlighting the 'beautiful scenery' and 'local colour', and so the Indian High Commission in London was none too pleased when they saw shots of Jeremy driving along in a Jaguar with a loo on the back, talking to locals dressed in his boxer shorts while using a trouser press and pinning signs to trains which ostensibly read, 'British IT is good for your company' and 'Eat English muffins', but turned into obscene messages when the trains parted. More complaints followed, especially from the IHC: 'The programme was replete with cheap jibes, tasteless humour and lacked the cultural sensitivity that we expect from the BBC.'

Yet again the Prime Minister got involved. At the start of the programme he was filmed waving to the trio and calling, 'Stay away from India.' Now he tried to distance himself as quickly as possible. The PM's spokesman said: 'Mr Cameron was leaving for an event when the cameras were there. This is a matter for the BBC.'

But then what did he expect? David Cameron was a personal friend of Jeremy's as well as a fan of the show, and no one who knew anything about Clarkson would be in too much doubt as to what might follow. It was hard to escape the conclusion that the PM was hoping a little bit of the Clarkson appeal would rub off on him when voters returned to the polling booth.

There was a lot of po-faced tutting along the lines that Jeremy was becoming a national liability, but this time the BBC refused to back down, aware that, for all the furious letter writers, there were millions of amused viewers. The corporation pointed out that the show had not been making fun of India itself, but of the presenters.

Nor did the fact that Jeremy seemed intent on insulting every country in the entire world seem to actually put the entire world off of him. His popularity even survived an appearance by Alex in front of a Commons privacy inquiry, in which she described how the injunction had terrified her. Clarkson's name was coming up pretty regularly in the House of Commons these days.

A charity called Changing Faces was the next to take umbrage, when Jeremy compared one car on *Top Gear* to 'people with growths on their faces', claiming that people 'wouldn't talk to [the car] at a party'. Indeed, it was getting increasingly difficult to find some section of society that Clarkson had not managed to insult. He had sparked so many controversies that his name quite frequently came up in discussions about free speech itself – the point being that if Jeremy Clarkson wasn't free to make a few harmless jokes (and most were ultimately harmless), then whither free speech?

But for all the controversy he caused, no one denied that Jeremy was an extremely talented broadcaster. In May 2012, he collected the Honorary Rose Award at the Rose D'Or Festival in Lucerne, joking as he did so that, 'Approximately seven million cars had to be destroyed to win this award.' In high spirits, he added, 'This is the best job in the world.'

Shrugging off another controversy as he went – immigration queues in airports would be lessened if only officials used a bit of racism, he'd joked – he then discovered himself to be subject to a police investigation into the alleged disturbance of protected barn owls. It was becoming surreal: this was the result of an appearance on *Countryfile*, not *Top Gear*, in which Jeremy and the completely uncontroversial Chris Packham were shown filming owls at Jeremy's country home.

But it was quite serious. A Barn Owl Trust spokesman confirmed: 'We are slightly concerned that the programme gave the impression that flushing pairs of birds from potential nest sites is a common occurrence. If the producers knew that the birds were not breeding and therefore that flushing them out was not an issue, it would have been good to have made this clear at the outset.'

It actually blew up into quite a row. Not to be outdone, PC Josh Marshall, Devon and Cornwall Police's wildlife crime officer, tweeted: 'Irresponsible to show that behaviour without warning people watching you need appropriate licences.'

Nevertheless the jibes continued to flow, with Jeremy having a pop at Andy Murray for crying in public – 'It's like eating a horse. Something that only foreigners do' – and the money continued to flow in. Named as the top-earning star at the BBC, it appeared his salary now amounted to more than £3 million a year.

There was, however, a rare case of the biter being bitten when Jeremy tweeted that his pet Labrador, Whoopi, had been put to sleep. He received a tirade of unpleasant remarks in return, which upset him so much that he felt moved to remind everyone the UK was the country that invented concentration camps and the international slave trade. He was only human, after all, and the Twitter sniping had come on top of a turbulent private life.

Still, the Clarkson coffers continued to fill. Jeremy sold his 30 per cent stake in Bedder 6 to the BBC for a cool £15 million in September 2012, at the same time renewing his three-year contract (as did James and Richard).

With interesting coincidental timing, one week later the BBC Trust upheld a complaint against Clarkson for the first time in four years: relating to the jibe about the Toyota Prius van looking like someone with a growth on their face (Clarkson called it the 'Elephant Car', in reference to the Elephant Man). 'Banter such as was broadcast on *Top Gear* would always be an imperfect science; it would invariably upset some viewers at some point,' said the show's executive producer, Andy Wilman. But if Jeremy was concerned, it certainly didn't show.

There was celebration in some quarters that he'd finally been tamed, but of course he hadn't at all. The *Top Gear Live* show turned up at Birmingham's NEC with larks a-plenty, including Clarkson's Ford Fiesta sling-shotted into a row of parked cars. Jeremy claimed he was risking death, but in the event got off with a slight gash to the leg. There was also a bubbly appearance on *Have I Got News For You*, followed by a sighting with Phillipa on holiday in Rome.

As 2012 drew to a close, there was much to celebrate. As bruising as the row with Alexandra had been, at least it was out in the open; he was wealthier than he'd ever been and remained extraordinarily popular. Life was good.

CHAPTER 15

CLARKSON RETAKES THE FALKLANDS

By the beginning of 2013, Jeremy's ability to cause controversy was such that he didn't even need to do anything to prompt it. Just being part of the Chipping Norton set, say, ensured that every time it got a mention (and due to the controversy surrounding fellow members David Cameron and Rebekah Wade, it got a lot of mentions) Jeremy's name bobbed up. Time and age was doing nothing to temper his opinions, either. He clearly enjoyed stirring up controversies, although he was on the verge of one that could have proved personally dangerous.

His importance to the BBC, alongside James and Richard, was highlighted by the fact that in 2013, *Top Gear* was named the world's most watched factual entertainment show, broadcast in 244 countries. 'It's become one of BBC Two's channel-defining shows,' said Chris Curtis, deputy editor of *Broadcast* magazine in an interview with the *Daily Express*, 'not just for its popularity but in the sense that it's got a personality, a point of view. It's one of those shows people love, but also love to hate a little bit.' But they really did love it. The trio of presenters were widely seen to be acting out middle-aged-male fantasies, and as the new series kicked off, viewers were promised a rugby game with the latest Kia hatchback, a voyage to the source of the Nile and an attempt to impress *Dragons' Den* with a micro vehicle, amidst much else. This wasn't just a show about cars – it was a show about doing exactly what you wanted while thumbing your nose at what society demands of your behaviour and being extremely entertaining en route.

Jeremy lost no time in giving the easily offended further cause for complaint (you had to wonder why they actually watched the programme) by using a car to draw a giant depiction of a male member in the Los Angeles desert, which prompted unpleasant comments on Twitter, after which Jeremy's own account was hacked. This did not stop him from posting a shot of him feasting on rabbits' ears when in Moscow, prompting complaints from animal rights activists. He was certainly globe trotting: he next turned up in Australia where a group of Ozzie photographers irritated him by snapping him with Phillipa ('You can take them out of England but you just can't take the convict out of them') before moving on to New Zealand, where he upset the Maori community by threatening to drive over a local sacred beach.

Back in Blighty he blamed jetlag on the Ozzie outburst (the locals hadn't taken the reference to convicts too well) but it was a mark of the fact that he now moved in the highest echelons of the establishment when it was revealed that he was on the guest list for Lady Thatcher's funeral. The current prime minister was a friend, after all, so it was no surprise when he was included among the great and good to say goodbye to another. ('We sang some hymns and listened to a Labour Party political broadcast from a bearded man in a frock' – this was a reference to the Right Rev. Richard Chartres, the Bishop of London, who gave an address some felt leaned a little to the left.) And he was, after all, a Conservative himself, something else which marked him out at the BBC.

Clarkson's next target was Puerto Rico and by association Sir Bruce Forsyth, whose wife came from the island – 'It may be a bit chilly in Britain but at least there's a chance of getting to the post office without having your watch nicked and your head cut off' – but given that it was now estimated that Jeremy had made about £14 million from deals with the BBC he could afford to ignore the aggro. Pausing only to infer that caravanners were 'doggers', Clarkson got his knuckles rapped when it turned out that restaurant diners soaked by Clarkson in a passing vehicle on *Top Gear* were in fact actors. Nothing abashed, he issued a fierce criticism of the BBC for running a documentary celebrating the German motor industry straight after an episode of *Top Gear* praising British cars. (Richard Hammond was pretty irritated, too.)

Politics were at the forefront again when Clarkson suggested he might take on Ed Miliband in the general election, although he later claimed he'd only tweeted about it because he was drunk, before speculation arose that he might stand against Nick Clegg instead. In truth, although many voters would have loved him, there was no way Jeremy could really be a politician – the fact that he was so capable of insulting large swathes of society without even thinking about it would have seen to that. Nor did his complicated personal life help – he had just been spotted with Phillipa in Greece.

He was better off doing what he did best – namely, broadcasting. And for all the *Top Gear* laddishness, Jeremy remained only too capable of tapping into public emotion and paying tribute to serious issues that chimed with the public. In December 2013, he made a documentary about the Arctic convoys between 1941 and 1945, in which about 3,000 Merchant and Royal Navy sailors were killed delivering supplies to the Soviet Union, which was fighting against Germany in the Second World War. 'I genuinely believe that the bravest men who ever lived are those who served on the convoys in the Second World War,' he said. 'To be shot at anywhere is scary but to be shot at hundreds of miles from land with no chance of rescue, amid mountainous waves, is really something quite different. These veterans are the bravest of the brave.' It was a sentiment with which many viewers could wholeheartedly agree and yet another illustration of the fact that Jeremy had an innate understanding of and bond with many Britons that was simply unmatched elsewhere on the BBC.

But Jeremy wouldn't be Jeremy without the ability to cause offence. When Michael Schumacher had a skiing accident that put him into a coma, Jeremy couldn't help himself. 'The worrying thing about brain injuries is that you can recover only to find you're a midget with a marked Birmingham accent when drunk,' he tweeted. This was a clear reference to Richard Hammond and his accident. Twitter went mad.

★　★　★

It was when Jeremy was in the middle of the 'eeny, meeny, miny, moe' controversy, in which there was intensive speculation as to whether had used the n-word, that he received the news that every child must dread. He was in the middle of a *Top Gear* Live tour in Russia when he received the news that his mother Shirley had died on 24 March 2014, aged seventy-nine, and it affected him badly: the two were very close. Shirley had had cancer. For all the bluster, Jeremy has a considerably softer side than he liked to let on and he later revealed that what he wanted to do on hearing the news was weep, because he had been very close to his mother. But if he'd done so, he said, the *Daily Mirror* would have run the pictures and claimed they were tears of shame. 'It was a gruesome time.'

And so, in what had been a very turbulent couple of years, Jeremy lost his surviving parent, the rite of passage that so many of us dread. There has been speculation that it was the breakdown of his marriage that sent him a little off the rails in recent times, drinking very heavily and finally going too far in punching his producer, of which more anon, but it is just as likely to have been the passing of his mother.

The two were once interviewed for the 'Relative Values' slot in *The Sunday Times* back in 2001 and their words showed how close they were. 'I was always a bit of a mother's boy,' wrote Jeremy. 'I can certainly see a lot of her in me – she's one of those life-and-soul-of-the party, bang-the-furniture, make-a-joke-about-anything characters. Which is very much the image people have of Jeremy Clarkson. Even when I was an idiot teenager, I was in awe of her and how she could hold the entire room with one of her stories. Her friends used to call them Clarkson stories; they were, like, these elaborately exaggerated anecdotes. I'm sure they thought she made them up.'

His mother, meanwhile, while clearly doting on her son, was already clearly concerned about becoming a burden to him. 'We deal with emotions by having a laugh,' she wrote. 'It's like when Jeremy comes to see me – the first thing he does is pat the cushions on my settee. "It's okay, Mother," he shouts, "you've not started wetting them yet!" We have this agreement: whenever I start dribbling my food or having accidents on the settee, he'll drive up to Beachy Head and push me over the edge. And it's mutual. I talk to a lot of Jeremy's friends and they always tell me how their mothers drive them up the wall. I think: "What is it we mothers do that drives our kids up the wall? A lot of us have our faculties and can still get about – you should count yourself lucky your mother's not in a home." I dread the thought of that happening to me. And I'd never move in with the kids – I never want to be a burden. If that's not possible, then, like I said, it's off to Beachy Head.'

In the event she died quietly at home, leaving full instructions as to the funeral she wanted and everything else as well. Her choice of music? 'Thank You For The Music' by Abba. If anyone wanted to look at where Jeremy's high spirits came from, they really didn't need to look much further than his very much-loved mum.

★ ★ ★

Jeremy was known for his high jinks and propensity to upset, but on one occasion he really did nearly go too far, possibly putting his own life in danger alongside those of his cohorts. And when the problems really began, he publicly complained that the BBC wasn't being very supportive. In hindsight it's possible to see that relations between Jeremy and Auntie really were beginning to strain.

The incident began on 17 September 2014, when Jeremy and the team flew out to Argentina to film a *Top Gear* special, under strict instructions from the BBC not to start anything. Right from the start everyone involved knew there was the potential for this to blow up in their faces: not only was Jeremy known for insulting whole countries at random, but in this case tensions had been mounting because Argentina had been making aggressive-sounding rumbles about the Falklands, the islands the British retook after the Argentinian invasion in 1982, when Mrs Thatcher was running the show. To a pugnacious bruiser like Jeremy – and, in fairness, the other two as well – to send him to Argentina at such a sensitive time was akin to dousing the situation with oil and handing him a box of matches. And an explosion duly followed.

It started quietly, though, or at least what passes for quietly in Jeremy's world. The team arrived and Jeremy tweeted an innocuous shot of a messy hotel bar with the message, 'I am going to fucking live here.' But it didn't take long for matters to kick off. Jeremy was driving a Porsche 1,350 miles down the Patagonian Highway, accompanied by James in a Lotus and Richard in a Mustang, but no one noticed Jeremy's licence plate, at first, at least. Then someone did. It was H982 FKL, seemingly a deliberate reference to the Falklands War in 1982. *Clarin*, the national newspaper, said, 'This is highly sensitive for Argentinians and Clarkson could have problems.' It was right.

The BBC insisted it was an 'absolute coincidence' and that the number had been on the car when it was bought in August. The car itself was hastily hidden near Ushuaia, the capital of Tierra del Fuego and the southernmost city in the world. 'To suggest that this car was either chosen for its number plate, or that an alternative number plate was substituted for the original, is completely untrue,' said *Top Gear*'s producer Andy Wilman, but given Jeremy's past history of insulting his host countries, the coincidence was an unfortunate one to say the least. The other number plates came in for scrutiny, too, and some locals believed that the 269 on Hammond's car was close to the 255 Britons killed in the conflict and 646 on May's was a reference to the 649 Argentinian dead.

Matters quickly turned very ugly. War veterans staged an angry demonstration outside the Arakur hotel in Ushuaia where the team was staying – Jeremy later wrote the three of them hid under the bed in a researcher's room – and matters got so out of hand it was deemed that lives were actually at risk. The trio decided to cut short their trip, abandon their cars and hotfoot it across the border to Chile, probably a sensible choice in the circumstances. The rest of the team followed shortly afterwards.

Jeremy was clearly shaken. 'I've been to Iraq and Afghanistan, but this was the most terrifying thing I've ever been involved in,' he told *The Sun* in an interview before all the crew had managed to get out. 'There were hundreds of them. They were hurling rocks and bricks at our cars. They were trying to attack us with pickaxe handles. They were even driving lorries at our convoy to force us into the crowds. They wanted to drag us out. They were shouting, "Burn their cars, burn them, burn the pirates." Make no mistake, they 100 per cent wanted to kill us. This is not some kind of jolly *Top Gear* jape – this was deadly serious.'

The plates had come to light after a two-week drive, when a group of youngsters saw it and flashed it up on Twitter, so often the scene of mass hysteria and condemnation, which was certainly the case here. As soon as the connection had been made everyone got angrier and angrier. 'When we saw people on Twitter getting upset we took the plate off,' Jeremy continued. 'But they still attacked us, so we made a break for it to our hotel in Ushuaia. We thought once we got there they'd ease off, but the mob just descended on the hotel and encircled us. State representatives came and ordered us out of the country. I am convinced the mob was state-organised. Elections are coming up and they want to look like they stood up to the English. James, Richard and I thought if we left, things might calm down for the rest of the crew. We got nine seats on a flight to Buenos Aires, took some of the female members of staff, and scuttled out of the back door.'

Martin Marcilla, a receptionist at the hotel, confirmed what had happened. 'They were very tense moments,' he said. 'The war veterans were furious and shouting insults. Police had to remove them. Luckily things didn't get too out of hand. They left the hotel just before 7.30pm. It was all very sudden and unexpected. They left by a service door and in such a hurry that they even forgot a computer.' The crew abandoned the cars shortly afterwards, telling the locals they could burn them if they liked.

Although there was a great deal of local triumphalism at having forced the bad guys out of the country, not everyone felt it had been handled very well. While there were plenty of people saying that Clarkson had at last had a taste of his own medicine, the mob scenes had been very ugly and many felt they had backfired. 'We have committed a great mistake with the violence,' said the mayor of Ushuaia. 'That never resolves anything and the impact it was going to have was not taken into account. Instead of talking today about a person who was trying to be clever, we're talking about the victimisation of that same person. Obviously I don't agree with violence, and smashing windows or a car wasn't necessary. I believe the people responsible made a big mistake when they decided to act in that manner because now the news is that they decided to smash up the cars instead of talking about the real issue. The clever Dick ends up becoming the victim of this situation. It's deplorable.

I would have preferred it if nothing had been damaged. And if the TV programme had come here without creating distrust like this because they would have helped the city become better known in Europe.'

Back in the UK, Our Boys were point blank insisting it had all been an unfortunate coincidence and that they had done nothing wrong, but another unfortunate discovery seemed to suggest otherwise. Investigating Clarkson's abandoned Porsche, the locals found another licence plate, which bore the legend BEII END. This wasn't looking good, but the BBC gamely rushed out another statement. 'The number plate was not used at any point during filming. It was originally intended to be in the programme's final scene, a game of car football, but that ending has changed.'

The Argentinians, unsurprisingly, were having none of it. One local official said: 'We know bellend... is often employed as an insult in England. We regard it as another insult to the people of Argentina.' Some also saw references to the *General Belgrano*, the cruiser sunk by the British with the loss of 323 Argentine lives.

The episode came very close to sparking an international incident, with the Argentinian ambassador to the UK giving a furious response and calling for an apology, and there were a lot of people of the opinion that this time Clarkson really had gone too far. There were calls for him to be booted out of the BBC and even Andy Wilman admitted it had been a challenging year. 'We walk a tightrope, sometimes we're going to fall off and if you do, I'm not a fan of their [the BBC's] reaction,' he said. 'They're like, "Can you be naughty between the hours of [8pm and 9pm], can you be naughty under these conditions?" Sometimes I feel they don't trust us at heart, but – apart from the very odd occasion – we can be trusted. We're knackered after last year because it was a horrible year. It was our – what did the Queen say? – our annus horribilis. Our appetite is still there. I hope and think we'll continue.'

Jeremy himself allowed it to be known that he didn't think the Director General, Tony Hall, had stood up for the team. But for now, they were all still going ahead.

CHAPTER 16

BUST UP

By the end of 2014, Jeremy had turned into an almost unique mixture of enfant terrible and national treasure. His bosses at the BBC patently didn't understand his wider appeal and indeed, were going to go on to take a disastrous decision about the show he had made so famous, but for now he was doing better than ever. Now estimated to be worth in the region of at least £50 million, he was one of television's great success stories.

But Jeremy needed some of the money, at least, for legal fees. That row over the footpath across his land on the Isle of Man had dragged on for five years, between 2005 and 2010, until he was forced to open it to the public by the high court. And his marriage finally came to an end after twenty-one years when Frances filed for divorce in 2014. 'She's done her penance,' his first wife Alex told the *Daily Telegraph*. 'It is her hard work that has made him into the idol he is today. Jeremy is the frontman but behind the scenes she was the swan paddling frantically beneath the surface. So she deserves every penny she gets – she worked for it.'

However, it was in March 2015 that the incident briefly mentioned in the last chapter occurred, one that led to Jeremy's ultimate parting from the BBC. It was widely felt that he had been extremely provocative for some time and it was only his enormous popularity – and the fact that *Top Gear* was a huge money earner for the BBC, selling all over the world – that had saved him so far. But there was still muttering about the potentially racist 'slope' incident in the background and when the crunch came, the BBC was not prepared to put itself on the line for Jeremy – a decision it almost certainly came to regret.

Strangely, for an incident that was to have such massive repercussions, no one has disputed the main gist of what happened, although some of the details vary in the telling. In March 2015, the team had been filming in Hawes, North Yorkshire, and after a long day filming, returned to the hotel. Jeremy wanted a steak for supper but the hotel chef had already gone home and he was offered soup and a plate of cold cuts instead. Clarkson flew into a rage; matters got completely out of hand and he ended up punching *Top Gear* producer Oisin Tymon in the face. According to the latter, Clarkson also called him a 'lazy Irish c★★★.' Tymon ended up in hospital.

Jeremy was to end up apologising to Tymon repeatedly and there was also ultimately a behind-the-scenes cash settlement involving both Jeremy and the BBC, which was estimated to be well over £100,000. In the immediate aftermath, however, there was uproar. Jeremy is a big man physically and Oisin isn't, but while there was widespread sympathy for the producer, there was also serious concern over Jeremy's future. He was immediately suspended from the BBC and even the then Prime Minister, David Cameron, got dragged into the row, saying, 'I don't know exactly what happened. He is a constituent of mine, he is a friend of mine, he is a huge talent. I see that he said he regrets some of what happened. All I would say – because he is a talent and he does amuse and entertain so many people, including my children who'll be heartbroken if *Top Gear* is taken off air – I hope this can be sorted out because it is a great programme and he is a great talent.'

The BBC, however, had had enough. Jeremy was suspended. The upcoming episode of *Top Gear* was not broadcast. There is a common belief that Jeremy was fired, but this is not true: rather, his contract was up at the end of that month. Originally, everyone had been in talks to renew it; this was not now going to happen.

But the public was up in arms. The North Yorkshire police made inquiries into what happened, but Oisin declined to press charges. Jeremy was forced to ask the show's fans to stop trolling Oisin as the incident was not his fault. A petition was launched to get the BBC to change its mind; it swiftly gained one million signatures and was taken to the door of Number 10 by a man dressed as The Stig. BBC Director-General Tony Hall received death threats and in yet another bizarre twist, within 24 hours of his suspension, the Russian state broadcaster

Zvezda approached Jeremy to ask him to front a motoring programme.

Jeremy, always so much closer to the actual viewers than the management top brass, realised faster than his erstwhile employer what a terrible mistake they had made. 'There was an eighteen-year waiting list to be in the audience of *Top Gear*, but the BBC has fucked themselves. It was a great show and they've fucked it up,' he said at a charity event in London's Roundhouse, although he later claimed he was joking.

Tony Hall released a statement about what had happened, which really just served to reveal that the BBC did not understand what it was about to do. It read:

It is with great regret that I have told Jeremy Clarkson today that the BBC will not be renewing his contract. It is not a decision I have taken lightly. I have done so only after a very careful consideration of the facts and after personally meeting both Jeremy and Oisin Tymon.

I am grateful to Ken MacQuarrie [Director of BBC Scotland] for the thorough way he has conducted an investigation of the incident on 4th March. Given the obvious and very genuine public interest in this I am publishing the findings of his report. I take no pleasure in doing so. I am only making them public so people can better understand the background. I know how popular the programme is and I also know that this decision will divide opinion. The main facts are not disputed by those involved. I want to make three points.

First – The BBC is a broad church. Our strength in many ways lies in that diversity. We need distinctive and different voices but they cannot come at any price. Common to all at the BBC have to be standards of decency and respect. I cannot condone what has happened on this occasion. A member of staff – who is a completely innocent party – took himself to Accident and Emergency after a physical altercation accompanied by sustained and prolonged verbal abuse of an extreme nature. For me a line has been crossed. There cannot be one rule for one and one rule for another dictated by either rank, or public relations and commercial considerations.

Second – This has obviously been difficult for everyone involved but in particular for Oisin. I want to make clear that no blame attaches to him for this incident. He has behaved with huge integrity throughout. As a senior producer at the BBC he will continue to have an important role within the organisation in the future.

Third – Obviously none of us wanted to find ourselves in this position. This decision should in no way detract from the extraordinary contribution that Jeremy Clarkson has made to the BBC. I have always personally been a great fan of his work and *Top Gear*. Jeremy is a huge talent. He may be leaving the BBC but I am sure he will continue to entertain, challenge and amuse audiences for many years to come.

The BBC must now look to renew *Top Gear* for 2016. This will be a big challenge and there is no point in

CLARKSON

pretending otherwise. I have asked Kim Shillinglaw to
look at how best we might take this forward over the
coming months. I have also asked her to look at how we
put out the last programmes in the current series.

Anyone familiar with what was really going on, however, would
have had no trouble in reading between the lines. The then
Director of BBC Television was Danny Cohen and it was
widely known that he and Jeremy were the polar opposites of
one another, Cohen being the very epitome of the metropolitan
elite and not a man who liked Jeremy's sense of humour and
constant inability to toe the line. He was thought to have
wanted Jeremy to go for years and now he had his way.

Jeremy was well aware of this. 'Danny and I were, and I suspect
will remain forever, very far apart on every single thing,' he told
The Times a year later. 'Normally, you could find some common
ground with somebody, but I think Danny and I could probably
only get on perfectly well so long as we absolutely never had to
think about each other for the rest of the time. Because I don't
mind anyone having an opinion that's different to mine, just so
long as they don't mind my opinion, either. So long as it doesn't
impinge on what I want to do.'

The fallout began. 'BBC please take him back,' tweeted his
daughter Em. 'He's started cooking.'

James May, who witnessed the whole thing was door-stepped
by *5 News* and asked if he supported Jeremy. 'In many ways no,
I have said many times before the man's a nob, but I quite like
him. It's all getting a bit ridiculous,' came the reply. What did he

266

understand had happened? 'Not very much, I was blind drunk.
No further comments – sorry.'

But May was being disingenuous. It was not just Jeremy's
contract that had come to an end: so had that of James and
Richard Hammond. And they were walking, too, something
that had become apparent almost immediately from 25 March,
the day it was announced that Jeremy's contract would not be
renewed. May promptly changed his Twitter account to 'former
Top Gear presenter'. It was pretty clear what he intended to do.

'Me and Hammond with a surrogate Jeremy is a non-starter.
It has to be the three of us,' he told *The Guardian*. 'I don't
think you could carry on with two people and put someone
in as the new Jeremy because they are not going to be the
new Jeremy. That would be short-sighted and I don't think
it would work. Virtually impossible.' He was right, of course,
and in a rather different situation a couple of years later, when
The Great British Bake Off moved from the BBC to Channel
4, most of the presenters on that show similarly felt they could
only work as a team.

Richard Hammond felt exactly the same and announced his
own decision on Twitter: 'To be clear amidst all this talk of us
"quitting" or not: there's nothing for me to "quit". Not about
to quit my mates anyway.' Executive producer Andy Wilman, a
long-term friend of Clarkson, also announced he was off and it
was announced that on 28 June that year the final shows would
air as a compilation hosted by Richard and James. And what to
do with the *Top Gear Live* stage shows? They would continue
under the heading of *Clarkson, Hammond and May Live* instead.

For all the brave face he put on it, for Clarkson this was a time of enormous upheaval. He had lost his mother, his marriage had broken up and now he had lost his show as well. And it was a crisis for the BBC, which was still being slow to grasp quite what they had lost. A high-profile search for a replacement team began with, with such unlikely names as Sue Perkins seriously up for consideration. It was a ludicrous suggestion – the BBC didn't seem to realise that replacing a wildly popular bloke's bloke with a right-on lesbian might not have been the most obvious move – but like so many others involved in the saga, she too received death threats. This time it was left to James May to tell the fans to put a stop to it.

Other names put forward included Dermot O'Leary, Philip Glenister and Jodie Kidd, but in the event the main presenter was announced as Chris Evans, another blokey bloke. There was some excitement when the *Friends* actor Matt LeBlanc was named as co-host and not a great deal of excitement at all when the rest of the line-up came through: Eddie Jordan, Chris Harris, German racing driver Sabine Schmitz and motor journalist Rory Reid.

Among reports of backstage rows, arguments and upheavals, the word was that the new show wouldn't be a patch on the old, and it was right. Once the programme aired, the reviews were pretty awful, with most of the criticism aimed at Evans, who was certainly no new Jeremy. He and Matt didn't seem to get on that well either, thus completely failing to supply the blokey camaraderie that had characterised the previous lot: indeed, after a somewhat ill thought-out stunt in which Matt performed 'donuts' near the Cenotaph, Chris issued a grovelling apology which made it clear he had nothing to do with what many people saw as being deeply disrespectful, and that it was down to Matt.

But of the two of them, Matt was far more popular and his style of presenting went down far better with the audience. After the end of the run, bowing to the inevitable, Evans resigned. There was some relief behind the scenes when Matt said he would stay on: he, Harris and Reid would become the programme's main presenters. The old magic was gone, but something might be salvaged after all, although by this time even the BBC had started to realise that they had chucked away the jewel in the crown, a jewel that was not going to be that easy to replace. And so *Top Gear* went on in its new format, fans disappointed that their heroes had gone – but their heroes, by this time had started to make other plans. So just where was Jeremy going to go next?

CHAPTER 17

TOP GEAR ON STEROIDS

It didn't take long. Three of the most popular presenters on the BBC, along with their executive producer Andy Wilman, were known to be looking for a new gig. They formed a production company called W Chump and Sons (surely an ironic name, not least because the four company cars were Reliant Robin three-wheelers) and started to look around. The signs were there from the start that *Top Gear* would run into terrible problems without them and so it had turned out, but even before the crisis surrounding their successors, Clarkson and co. had found their new home. And given how much television had changed since the early days of *Top Gear*, it was fitting that their new channel would reflect this change, too.

For, of course, it wasn't a channel, or not in the traditional sense, at least. It was Amazon Prime. For some years before the boys left the BBC, one huge change in the way people watched programmes had been the rise of streaming services, online sites which started by taking older television shows and re-screening them and, as they grew in wealth and influence, commissioning their own series. At the time of writing, this has become commonplace, with hugely successful series commissioned especially for Netflix, such as *The Crown*, but even in mid-2015 it was something people were getting used to. Clarkson put it in his own inimitable way: 'I feel like I've climbed out of a biplane and into a spaceship.'

'Amazon? Oh yes. I have already been there. I got bitten by a bullet ant,' said an overexcited Richard.

'We have become part of the new age of smart TV. Ironic, isn't it?' asked James.

'They'll give us the freedom to make the programme we want ... there's a budget to produce programmes of the quality we want and this is the future,' said Andy Wilman in an interview with the *Radio Times*. It would have 'themes people will be familiar with. I can't tell you how good it feels to get the chance to produce something from scratch. We're all really excited. No one telling us what we can and can't do, just us hopefully producing great programmes. It feels really liberating.'

Much as Jeremy enjoyed his feuds, however, on this occasion he decided to forego one. He and Chris Evans were both larger-than-life characters and Jeremy was watched like a hawk to see if he would say anything disobliging about his successor. He held his peace. As rumours circulated about behind-the-scenes rows at *Top Gear* and about power struggles between producers and presenters, all three of the boys kept out of it and concentrated on the new show. Wilman, too, claimed he was not interested in a head-to-head between the two shows: 'The child in me probably would, but actually all the scheduling competition stuff is becoming irrelevant,' he told *Broadcast* magazine. 'People will watch programmes when they want to and not when they're told to. This is very much the future of how we'll watch TV.'

There were only a few moments when Jeremy let rip and then it seemed to be as much on the back of personal hurt as anything else: 'I was having a tricky year, and I was quite stressy,' he said in an interview on the BBC with Jonathan Ross, referring to the run-up to leaving. 'It was really hard. It was getting harder and harder to do that show, because it was getting bigger and bigger all the time. The problems were getting bigger and bigger, the lack of support was appalling, home life was difficult, they were very stressy times.' It was known that while the 'slope-gate' inquiry was rumbling on that Jeremy's mother had died; no one, it seems, had let up on the questioning and even for Jeremy it had become too much.

As for the new *Top Gear*, he was remarkably restrained. 'You look at the TV show, you read all the credits, you'll see the cameraman, the sound recordist, you'll see their names …You find me one where it says "written by". They just cobble it together,' he said to the BBC. 'Writing is everything.'

But there were issues to be aware of when it came to the new *Top Gear* and the new Amazon programme. There were any number of legal constraints to worry about: for a start they couldn't use the same format and they also couldn't use the word "gear". But they could make a programme about cars. No one, however, was unduly concerned about what was to come. Certainly *Top Gear* fans, disillusioned about what had happened to their show, could hardly wait. 'Star the smoke,' tweeted Jeremy. 'We have a name.' That name turned out to be *The Grand Tour*, a reference to the eighteenth- and nineteenth-century practice in which members of the British well-off would make a 'grand tour' throughout Europe; in this case it emerged that the show would come from different towns and countries in every episode.

'After months of deliberation and lots of useful suggestions from the public, for which the guys are very grateful, Jeremy Clarkson, Richard Hammond and James May have decided that, because they are taking their new Amazon Prime Show around the world, it will be called *The Grand Tour*,' a statement on their website read. 'Not only will the guys travel to different locations, but for the first time ever the studio audience recordings will travel every week, all housed within a giant tent. Amazon customers will have the chance to be in the audience when tickets are released through prize draws this summer.' They were signed up for an initial three series of twelve one-hour episodes. Interest began to rise.

Of course, this was an enormous coup for Amazon Prime as well. To land this particular trio was not only a publicity coup: it almost certainly meant that Clarkson fans would be signing up for Amazon Prime, thus massively widening its subscriber base. 'Customers told us they wanted to see the team back on screen, and we are excited to make that happen,' said Jay Marine, vice president of Amazon Prime Video in Europe. 'Millions of Prime members are already enjoying our ground-breaking original shows. We can't wait to see what Jeremy, Richard, James and the team will create in what is sure to be one of the most globally anticipated shows of 2016. This is a golden age of television, a great time for TV makers and storytellers. Our approach is to give programme makers creative freedom to be innovative and make the shows they want to make. This is just the start, you should expect to see more world-leading talent and the biggest shows on Prime Video.' There was another difference, too: according to some industry reports, the show was going to cost Amazon more than a quarter of a billion dollars. They were, 'very, very, very expensive', for Amazon said its CEO Jeff Bezos. 'They're worth a lot and they know it.' So, stakes were high.

There would be one small difference from other new shows on the streaming channels. Most were released in box-set form, with all the episodes going on air at once. This was not quite the case with *The Grand Tour*: rather, the first episode was to debut on 18 November 2016 and follow-ups released weekly after that to Amazon customers in the UK, US, Germany, Australia and Japan. After December 2016 it was to be made available to an additional 195 countries. No exact figures were given but Amazon said that the show was the most watched premiere in its history and that on the same day a record number of Amazon subscriptions were sold: 'The guys are back, doing what they do best – the chemistry between Jeremy, Richard, and James is what makes *The Grand Tour* so entertaining,' said Jeff Bezos. 'Their creativity, along with the amazing production quality and 4K HDR streaming, has Prime members responding in a big way. Kudos and congrats to the whole team.'

The show did indeed broadcast from various different parts of the globe, including Johannesburg, California, Nashville, Whitby, Lapland, Rotterdam and more. The show featured a large tent for studio segments, a test track called the Eboladrome because, according to Jeremy, it resembled the structure of the Ebola virus, and a test car driver in the shape of Mike Skinner. Running jokes included a drone being destroyed in the opening titles, the presenters' names being regularly misspelled and a joke about killing off the celebrity guests.

But Jeremy did admit to nerves. 'It troubles me, actually,' he said at a press call before the series began. I lie awake at night going, "It's just a car show", because there's been a lot of talk of massive budgets, and everybody is expecting the first programme to come from Jupiter, and for us all to have Iron Man suits and for it to be *The Avengers*. It isn't. It's three middle-aged men falling over.'

He need not have worried. The reviews were on the whole positive: 'Jeremy Clarkson and co leave the BBC in their dust,' said *The Guardian*. The first episode 'resembled a Hollywood blockbuster,' said the *Daily Express*, adding, '[*The Grand Tour* is] basically *Top Gear* on steroids.

The BBC, possibly still smarting at recent events, was not so generous. Arts editor, Will Gompertz commented, 'There is no irony [in the opening sequence.] It feels uncomfortably hubristic', but when the presenters were in situ, 'Normal service has been resumed... It seemed to me that *Grand Tour* is a TV show that wants to be – and quite possibly should be – a movie.' *The Independent* meanwhile said *The Grand Tour* was 'the best of *Top Gear* but with a greater budget'.

They were a little more negative the following week, which featured an SAS-style training session in Jordan. It was, said the *Daily Telegraph*, '[…] a tedious action movie segment suggested that they were in danger of losing the run of themselves slightly and that Amazon's hands-off policy towards the production had potential downsides.' And the *Radio Times* also felt that 'many of the viewers were disgruntled to say the least, branding the show as dull and not funny.'

Meanwhile it was actually Richard Hammond who managed to create the show's first controversy, when he implied that men who eat ice cream are gay (admittedly, a somewhat bizarre conclusion). He was criticised by Stonewall, gay rights campaigner Peter Tatchell and singer Olly Alexander, until it emerged that it was actually an in-joke for the Finnish audience as it referred to a controversial Finnish TV commercial.

Jeremy is not usually seen as an overly sensitive person, but in an interview with *The Times Magazine*, he revealed that even he could be hurt by the turn of events. 'My luck stopped suddenly,' he said of the interval between *Top Gear* and *The Grand Tour*. Apart from the BBC episode and the death of his mother, he also had to move out of the family home in the wake of the divorce and split up from his girlfriend Phillipa Sage. According to the great man himself, he temporarily gave up drinking, had a few early nights and even started some yoga first thing in the morning. At one point matters got so dark that during a scuba-diving session in a swimming pool, he spent the best part of the day at the bottom of the pool with an oxygen tank. 'It was so peaceful down there. Why would I want to come out?' he asked. But it didn't take long for the old Jeremy to come back. There was, however, more difficult news to come at the end of 2016 when his close friend Adrian Gill passed away on 10 December. Gill had revealed his terminal cancer diagnosis, or 'the full English' of cancer as he called it, in his *Sunday Times* column less than three weeks before. Jeremy was, as one might expect, devastated by the loss and wrote a moving piece in the *Sunday Times* a week later titled 'O Adrian, who will make me laugh now?'.

Whatever the future for *The Grand Tour*, the futures of its presenters were assured. They were very rich men and never needed to work again. But Jeremy's private life continued to fascinate: by early 2017, he had found a new girlfriend, Irish actress Lisa Hogan, ten years his junior. Lisa, who had previously been married to a millionaire playboy called Baron Bentinck, nephew of the billionaire Baron Heini von Thyssen, with whom she had three children, told *The Mirror*: 'I'm very happy. He's great.' They were seen together in Barbados; at 6ft 2 she was still not as tall as her new beau. Lisa had once caught the eye of John Cleese and had appeared in 1997 in *Fierce Creatures*, a film he co-wrote, as the sea-lion keeper. She had also once been involved in a plane crash when the Lear jet she was travelling in overshot the runway at RAF Northolt and crashed into the A40. Lisa emerged unscathed and as she later pointed out, she'd been in just the one crash; Jeremy had managed three.

Jeremy's urge to annoy had not entirely evaporated, however. In early 2017 he attended a gala dinner at the Roundhouse at which the BBC's top man Tony Hall was present: 'Two years ago I was working for the BBC – I know the director general is sitting over there now s★★★ing himself, but don't worry Tony, it's fine,' he said in a speech as he presented a prize in the charity auction. 'I came on this stage to offer an auction prize and I may have said some choice words about some of the BBC management. I was then sacked. As a result of that I've done really well for myself and now I'm at Amazon.' This was not actually his usual spiel: Jeremy preferred to point out that he had not been sacked. It was merely a case that his contract had not been renewed.

Lisa was in attendance that night. Did she look set to become wife number three? Only time would tell. His ex-wife Frances was also seen on holiday with a new man and also in Barbados, causing some amusement among onlookers, who pointed out that he was younger and considerably slimmer than her ex. *Top Gear* limped back into a second series, now fronted by Matt LeBlanc; he received a considerably better reception than Chris had, but it was clear the glory days were long gone. 'The *Top Gear* format is a classic piece of portmanteau television, but it should have been parked when the BBC made the unnecessary, politically motivated and financially ruinous decision to fire Jeremy Clarkson,' wrote *GQ* editor Dylan Jones. 'Instead the producers have once again drafted in a generic celebrity and two Muggles who both look as though they have spent formative parts of their career working in local radio or children's TV.'

In April 2017, Jeremy turned fifty-seven, but although he had not lost his power to shock, there was almost something of the grand old man about him rather than the enfant terrible now. He still had his columns in both *The Sun* and *The Sunday Times* and he seemed happier now at Amazon than he had been at the Beeb. 'When you send Amazon a film, their television people in Los Angeles ring up and squeak with joy,' he told Jonathan Ross. 'What you never get at the BBC is that – ever. Because if somebody was to say, "That was a great thing that you've just done", particularly if they wrote it in an email, if it turned out to be controversial and the *Daily Mail* went berserk, they'd be on record as having liked it, and then what would happen? It's a terrible culture, and all of Britain suffers from it.'

Jeremy, however, appeared to have broken free from it. It was time for the next chapter of his life.